HOW TO COPE WITH PEOPLE
WHO DRIVE YOU CRAZY

DR PAUL HAUCK is a full-time clinical psychologist in Rock Island, Illinois, USA. He is a fellow of the American Psychological Association, and has lectured widely on various aspects of psychology. He has written many articles for professional journals, and his books (which have been translated into 16 languages) include *Calm Down, Jealousy, How to Stand up for Yourself, How to Do What You Want to Do, How to Love and Be Loved, Depression, How to Be Your Own Best Friend* and *Hold Your Head Up High* – all published by Sheldon Press.

Overcoming Common Problems Series

For a full list of titles please contact
Sheldon Press, Marylebone Road, London NW1 4DU

The Assertiveness Workbook
A plan for busy women
JOANNA GUTMANN

Beating the Comfort Trap
DR WINDY DRYDEN AND JACK
GORDON

Birth Over Thirty Five
SHEILA KITZINGER

Body Language
How to read others' thoughts by their
gestures
ALLAN PEASE

Body Language in Relationships
DAVID COHEN

Calm Down
How to cope with frustration and anger
DR PAUL HAUCK

Cancer – A Family Affair
NEVILLE SHONE

The Candida Diet Book
KAREN BRODY

Caring for Your Elderly Parent
JULIA BURTON-JONES

Cider Vinegar
MARGARET HILLS

Comfort for Depression
JANET HORWOOD

Coping Successfully with Hayfever
DR ROBERT YOUNGSON

**Coping Successfully with Joint
Replacement**
DR TOM SMITH

Coping Successfully with Migraine
SUE DYSON

Coping Successfully with Pain
NEVILLE SHONE

Coping Successfully with Panic Attacks
SHIRLEY TRICKETT

Coping Successfully with PMS
KAREN EVENNETT

**Coping Successfully with Prostate
Problems**
ROSY REYNOLDS

**Coping Successfully with Your Hiatus
Hernia**
DR TOM SMITH

**Coping Successfully with Your Irritable
Bowel**
ROSEMARY NICOL

**Coping Successfully with Your Irritable
Bladder**
JENNIFER HUNT

Coping with Anxiety and Depression
SHIRLEY TRICKETT

Coping with Blushing
DR ROBERT EDELMANN

Coping with Breast Cancer
DR EADIE HEYDERMAN

Coping with Bronchitis and Emphysema
DR TOM SMITH

Coping with Candida
SHIRLEY TRICKETT

Coping with Chronic Fatigue
TRUDIE CHALDER

Coping with Coeliac Disease
KAREN BRODY

Coping with Cystitis
CAROLINE CLAYTON

Coping with Depression and Elation
DR PATRICK McKEON

Coping with Eczema
DR ROBERT YOUNGSON

Coping with Endometriosis
JO MEARS

Coping with Fibroids
MARY-CLAIRE MASON

Coping with a Hernia
DR DAVID DELVIN

Coping with Psoriasis
PROFESSOR RONALD MARKS

Coping with Rheumatism and Arthritis
DR ROBERT YOUNGSON

Coping with Stammering
DR TRUDY STEWART AND JACKIE
TURNBULL

Coping with Stomach Ulcers
DR TOM SMITH

Overcoming Common Problems Series

Coping with Thrush
CAROLINE CLAYTON

Coping with Thyroid Problems
DR JOAN GOMEZ

Coping with Your Cervical Smear
KAREN EVENNETT

Crunch Points for Couples
JULIA COLE

Curing Arthritis
More ways to a drug-free life
MARGARET HILLS

Curing Arthritis Diet Book
MARGARET HILLS

Curing Arthritis – The Drug-Free Way
MARGARET HILLS

Curing Arthritis Exercise Book
MARGARET HILLS AND JANET
HORWOOD

Depression
DR PAUL HAUCK

Divorce and Separation
Every woman's guide to a new life
ANGELA WILLANS

**Everything Parents Should Know About
Drugs**
SARAH LAWSON

Feverfew
DR STEWART JOHNSON

Gambling – A Family Affair
ANGELA WILLANS

Garlic
KAREN EVENNETT

The Good Stress Guide
MARY HARTLEY

Heart Attacks – Prevent and Survive
DR TOM SMITH

**Helping Children Cope with Attention
Deficit Disorder**
DR PATRICIA GILBERT

Helping Children Cope with Bullying
SARAH LAWSON

Helping Children Cope with Divorce
ROSEMARY WELLS

Helping Children Cope with Dyslexia
SALLY RAYMOND

Helping Children Cope with Grief
ROSEMARY WELLS

Hold Your Head Up High
DR PAUL HAUCK

How to Be Your Own Best Friend
DR PAUL HAUCK

How to Cope When the Going Gets Tough
DR WINDY DRYDEN AND JACK
GORDON

How to Cope with Anaemia
DR JOAN GOMEZ

How to Cope with Bulimia
DR JOAN GOMEZ

How to Cope with Difficult Parents
DR WINDY DRYDEN AND JACK
GORDON

How to Cope with Difficult People
ALAN HOUEL WITH CHRISTIAN
GODEFROY

**How to Cope with People who Drive You
Crazy**
DR PAUL HAUCK

How to Cope with Splitting Up
VERA PEIFFER

How to Cope with Stress
DR PETER TYRER

How to Enjoy Your Retirement
VICKY MAUD

How to Improve Your Confidence
DR KENNETH HAMBLY

How to Interview and Be Interviewed
MICHELE BROWN AND GYLES
BRANDRETH

How to Keep Your Cholesterol in Check
DR ROBERT POVEY

How to Love and Be Loved
DR PAUL HAUCK

How to Pass Your Driving Test
DONALD RIDLAND

How to Stand Up for Yourself
DR PAUL HAUCK

**How to Start a Conversation and Make
Friends**
DON GABOR

How to Stick to a Diet
DEBORAH STEINBERG AND
DR WINDY DRYDEN

How to Stop Worrying
DR FRANK TALLIS

How to Untangle Your Emotional Knots
DR WINDY DRYDEN AND JACK
GORDON

How to Write a Successful CV
JOANNA GUTMANN

Overcoming Common Problems Series

Hysterectomy
SUZIE HAYMAN

The Incredible Sulk
DR WINDY DRYDEN

The Irritable Bowel Diet Book
ROSEMARY NICOL

The Irritable Bowel Stress Book
ROSEMARY NICOL

Is HRT Right for You?
DR ANNE MACGREGOR

Jealousy
DR PAUL HAUCK

Learning to Live with Multiple Sclerosis
DR ROBERT POVEY, ROBIN DOWIE
AND GILLIAN PRETT

Living with Angina
DR TOM SMITH

Living with Asthma
DR ROBERT YOUNGSON

Living with Diabetes
DR JOAN GOMEZ

Living with Grief
DR TONY LAKE

Living with High Blood Pressure
DR TOM SMITH

Living with a Stoma
DR CRAIG WHITE

Making the Most of Yourself
GILL FOX AND SHEILA DAINOW

Menopause
RAEWYN MACKENZIE

The Migraine Diet Book
SUE DYSON

Motor Neurone Disease – A Family Affair
DR DAVID OLIVER

The Nervous Person's Companion
DR KENNETH HAMBLY

Out of Work – A Family Affair
ANNE LOVELL

Overcoming Anger
DR WINDY DRYDEN

Overcoming Shame
DR WINDY DRYDEN

Overcoming Stress
DR VERNON COLEMAN

The Parkinson's Disease Handbook
DR RICHARD GODWIN-AUSTEN

The PMS Diet Book
KAREN EVENNETT

Second Time Around
ANNE LOVELL

Serious Mental Illness – A Family Affair
GWEN HOWE

Sex & Relationships
ROSEMARY STONES

The Stress Workbook
JOANNA GUTMANN

The Subfertility Handbook
VIRGINIA IRONSIDE AND SARAH
BIGGS

Talking About Anorexia
How to cope with life without starving
MAROUSHKA MONRO

Ten Steps to Positive Living
DR WINDY DRYDEN

Think Your Way to Happiness
DR WINDY DRYDEN AND JACK
GORDON

**Understanding Obsessions and
Compulsions**
A self-help manual
DR FRANK TALLIS

Understanding Your Personality
Myers-Briggs and more
PATRICIA HEDGES

Overcoming Common Problems

How to Cope with People Who Drive You Crazy

Dr Paul Hauck

First published in Great Britain in 1998 by
Sheldon Press, SPCK, Marylebone Road, London NW1 4DU

© Dr Paul Hauck 1998

British Library Cataloguing-in-Publication Data
A catalogue for this book is available from the British Library

ISBN 0–85969–794–0

Photoset by Deltatype Limited, Birkenhead, Merseyside
Printed in Great Britain by
Biddles Ltd, Guildford and King's Lynn

Contents

Acknowledgements   ix
Introduction   1

1 The wrong client   3
2 Control freaks   14
3 The bullies   31
4 The brats   48
5 The losers   59
6 Slobs, neatniks and pests   72
7 Finishing touches   83

References and further reading   97

Acknowledgements

Never have four secretaries devoted so much time to the revisions of any manuscript I have ever written. Through it all they have been patient, smiling and good humoured.

Thank you Pamlyn Hunt, Dana Miller, Natasha Liezert and Jody Longman for your cooperation.

I also dedicate this book to the many professionals who have worked hard over the years to make Rational-Emotive Behaviour Therapy (REBT) grow. It is now an international movement. I was fortunate to be part of it in the early days when I was introduced to this system and first met Albert Ellis and Robert Harper at Temple University, Philadelphia in 1964.

Shortly thereafter Dr Ellis moved to his present quarters, The Institute for Rational Emotive Therapy New York City, where he gathered a staff of capable people who distinguished themselves over the ensuing 31 years to make REBT a respectable and vital force within the psychotherapeutic community.

The persons to whom I am most grateful for keeping this movement alive and well are many, but I want to give special recognition to those with whom I am personally familiar. I tip my cap to:

Albert Ellis: for his energy and incredible devotion to the movement. Without him it would not have happened.

Robert Harper: one of the earliest adherents and pioneers of REBT and co-author of one of the best books on the subject: *A New Guide to Rational Living*.

Janet Wolff: the current director of the New York Institute and an influential speaker and author, especially on the psychology of women.

Raymond Digiuseppe and Dominic Dimattia: both long-standing professional staffers at the New York Institute. They are accomplished speakers, writers and researchers and have left their stamp on REBT.

Windy Dryden: of the University of London, has written voluminously in a lucid and easy style which has furthered REBT in Britain as well as in the United States.

Terry London: a teacher, author and therapist who revitalized the Institute for Rational Emotive Therapy in Chicago.

Virginia Ann Church: was active in the Institute in New York, but especially in the Institutes in Clearwater, Florida and San Francisco, California.

Vincent Parr and Robert Moore: have kept the Clearwater Institute active in the south through an active outpatient centre and radio and television presentations.

Russel Grieger and Paul Wood: co-editors of the *Journal of Rational Emotive and Cognitive Behavior Therapy*, who turned my 1965 unsophisticated version of the journal, *Rational Living*, into a first-class professional publication, with heavy emphasis on research.

Michael Bernard: of Melbourne, Australia has edited excellent texts by outstanding REBT thinkers and helped spread the word Down Under. He is also the current editor of the revitalized *Journal of Rational Emotive and Cognitive Behavior Therapy*.

Maxie Maultsby: for his creative talents which brought forth his version of therapy: Rational Behavior Therapy, plus his organization International Association of Clear Thinkers (IACT).

Finally, my thanks to Glenda Hicks, PhD, and her husband Ray, of South Africa who lured me to that wonderful land in 1991 to present six seminars in Johannesburg and one in Cape Town, and again in 1995 at Witts University, Johannesburg.

I salute these colleagues for their contributions to the organization of REBT as well for their own unique professional contributions as clinicians.

Teresa
Alexander
Will
Grant

Introduction

Here I am, pen in hand, writing an introduction to a book I swore never to write. I made the very same pledge with the two before this one, but again, I am obsessed with the gnawing feeling deep within that, pledge or not, I have something to say which is too important to take to the grave.

Does this sound grandiose, conceited, boastful? I certainly hope not. I have long since received all the honours and recognition as a psychologist, writer and lecturer I could want. Granted, I am not a household name, but I have achieved a measure of recognition worldwide among select and interested professional and lay groups far beyond my dreams.

No, this has nothing to do with an ego trip. I am writing this book not because I want to but because I feel compelled to. Writing is a draining experience. It leaves little space for lighthearted reading. I can't read novels, poetry, history or science, at least outside my own field, if I have a book floating around in my head. When I am into my innermost thoughts about chapter headings, the content of each chapter, or the examples I shall use to make my points, I can assure you I sometimes am in a semi-trance and appear to be carrying on a conversation, when in fact I am staring right through the speaker, not hearing a word. My wife has quite rightly more than once been cross with me for not laying my professional concerns aside when I am home.

No matter. It's the price a writer pays for the creation of a book. It can't proceed by the clock, it wanders like a river, at its own pace and in unexpected directions. A good example of this last point is the very act of my writing this introduction. I intended it to be the beginning of Chapter 1. Instead, in a mysterious way, which I can't account for, I suddenly decided to begin this book with these remarks.

So, to get back to my original question of why I am writing my fifteenth book, the answer is clearly that I have perceived a human condition which is so disturbing and painful that it must be addressed. But more, this condition is poorly understood and poorly dealt with.

1

Therefore, in this, probably my last book, I want to confront this issue in an open and fearless manner, something which has not been done concerning a group of people I refer to as the crazymakers. As you shall soon learn in greater detail, these people are everywhere, create disruption wherever they interact and, worst of all, are not only tolerated in some quarters, but admired.

We have all been victimized at one time or another by a crazymaker, and sometimes we ourselves have been crazymakers. To make you aware of this condition, the way it functions, the forms it takes, how it affects us and how we can cope with it is the precise purpose of this book.

1
The wrong client

In my 43 years as a clinical psychologist I have had the good fortune to study human nature in detail and in its infinite variety and complexity. Great satisfaction was my reward when troubled persons gained understanding and control of those habits which brought them to me. The emphasis of my counselling was to show the clients how they were upsetting themselves and what they needed to stop that practice. In this way I, and thousands of counsellors throughout the world, have helped people reduce or almost eliminate the pains of crushing guilt, dangerous anger, trembling fear, raging jealousy or debilitating procrastination. Servicing these personal needs of our clients was considered our proper domain of operation. Even when we called in the partners, parents, children, employers or teachers of our clients, this was only done with the thought in mind of giving the client greater understanding and speeding up the pace of counselling.

Two sources of emotional problems

Picture yourself on a golf course. You're alone, practising the swing that would produce a long drive. Time after time, however, you hit the ball so that it curves left, then right, or is top-spinned and falls short. That long, arching shot straight down the fairway just isn't materializing.

What's wrong? It's not the weather: the sun is out and it's a warm day. The air is quiet and couldn't be diverting your ball from a straight flight. You're all by yourself, so we can't blame others for distracting you. In short, what's wrong is your poor playing. The problem can't be attributed to anyone but you.

You realize that easily and quickly. And then you decide to get upset. A vast array of choices lies before you, like a counter full of fruits at the supermarket. You can get depressed, feel guilty, pity yourself, feel inferior, become suspicious and even paranoid, get angry, jealous, envious, worried or panicky – any one of these, and more. They are disturbances you could give to yourself. Technically, they are known as intrapsychic disturbances.

Now, suppose you were playing just as badly as I have already described, but you're with three people, another male and two females. They naturally kid you about the balls you hit into the rough, and then they place their shots straight down the fairway, just like that. Again you get upset, but this time mainly in response to the kidding you're getting. You could get just as depressed, angry, nervous and envious in this situation as you did in the former. However, this time the disturbance is caused by you over the indirect influence of others, and this we call an interpsychic disorder.

I make this distinction at some length because most of our unhappiness does not come from intrapsychic problems, when we alone upset ourselves. On the contrary, most human disorders come from our reactions to the treatment we receive from others, the interpsychic reactions. This is what I repeatedly observed since my earliest days as a clinical psychologist. People generally had difficulties with others and less often with themselves. And where were these troublemakers? The only three places they could be: at home, at work or in the community.

Repeatedly I would ask my clients if I might also speak with their partners, relatives, children, parents, neighbours or employers to see if progress might be made more rapidly. Sometimes they would consent to see me. When this happened I was usually able to obtain a clearer picture of the dynamics of my client. Sometimes I learned how overly sensitive my client was. At other times I was immediately able to see the full extent of the unkind and threatening behaviour to which he or she had been subjected.

When this happened I realized my client was often a minor actor in the drama we were involved in. The 'invisible frustrator' is the one I should have been dealing with all along. He's the one who physically abused my client, called him ugly names and shamed him at every turn. She's the young girl who screamed at her passive mother, accusing the elderly lady of being selfish and uncaring and who must make more sacrifices for her daughter or the hysterics will continue for hours. It was the invisible frustrator who took control over his wife to such a degree that she learned not to think for herself, lost her confidence to make the simplest decisions, began to drink, and who was then referred to me for psychotherapy by her dominating husband who indirectly contributed to this problem in the first place.

Theme after theme given to me by my clients of their loss of self-esteem, their thoughts of suicide, their rages whose fires could

4

temporarily be quenched only by alcohol, helped me see the full picture, to complete the equation of human disturbance which led me to refer to them as the crazymakers, and to the writing of this book.

The equation I referred to might sum up my perceptions in the following manner:

UP + CM × F × I × D = DP
UP (undisturbed person/s) plus CM (crazymaker/s), multiplied by F, the frequency, I, the intensity and D, the duration of the meanness = DP (disturbed person/s).

This realization should bring considerable relief to many of you. When you were inclined to believe your distress was mainly your fault, I wish to suggest that first, you are at least 51 per cent directly responsible for your troubled feelings. No one can upset you emotionally unless you allow them to. All the crazymakers in the world can't, just by themselves, drive you crazy. You, the one who's depressed, angry or fearful, are the major cause of your neurotic feelings. You are not responsible for the frustrations crazymakers give you. You are responsible for how you respond to them.

The other side of the coin makes the crazymakers no more than 49 per cent indirectly responsible for your emotional pains since they can't directly hurt you unless they hurt you physically. In that case, they're 100 per cent responsible for your pains.

That being the case, why am I bothering to write this book about crazymakers when they're not actually responsible for your emotional upsets? In a manner of speaking, they're the carriers of craziness. People, being people, will usually respond to frustrations with disturbed feelings. Often they're harmless emotions such as disappointment, regret or sadness. However, when reactions reach the level of fury, suicide or anxiety attacks, they're responding intensely to frustrations, which they would not normally do if they were confronted with lesser annoyances.

Who are these people?

They come in all degrees of disturbance. Some are harmless slobs who never pick up after themselves and let their dishes pile up in their kitchen sinks. You can imagine what joy that brings to the neatnik partner the slob lives with.

From this comical couple the seriousness of their behaviour goes up as we study the spoiled brats of the world, then the losers, the control freaks and, worst of all, the bullies, the worst of all the crazymakers. These will be dealt with in greater detail in the following pages, although in reverse order.

Crazymakers come from all walks of life. Every business has impossible bosses, supervisors and directors. They can just as easily live in your neighbourhood. But the worst place to find them is right there in your home. Crazymakers also come from the ranks of partners, parents and children. They come from both sexes, all ages, all educational levels and all social classes. They're everywhere. But, never forget, they include you and me also from time to time.

For practical reasons I can't describe the vast majority of crazymakers; that would make a book so big you wouldn't want to read it. Instead, I'll focus on several personalities that are so common and upsetting that we all need to know how to identify and to cope with them.

These are people who learned certain habits as young adults and did it so thoroughly that they're now very difficult to change. That's precisely why they're more likely to be called crazymakers than others who do not habitually annoy their fellow man. They're rigid, self-righteous and don't care what others think of them.

What makes crazymakers?

Personality is developed in two ways: first, through learning, and second, through physical and/or genetic makeup. Learning can result from what we're all taught as our parents raised us. Some of us had parents who were hardworking, spent money wisely, were gentle and responsible. That helped us to grow into mature and stable adults, and it was achieved primarily through modelling. As the saying goes, 'The apple does not fall far from the tree.' Commonsense tells us that we learn without realizing that we're learning. Behaviours of neatness, kindness, honesty and responsibility, because we see them so often and adopt them for ourselves, teach us to model them. That's how we learn to speak the language of our guardians. Can you imagine for a moment a child from Italian parents growing up in Italy speaking only Russian?

Just as positive character traits are transmitted by learning, so too are the negative traits. Parents who solve every dispute with screaming and name-calling teach their children those habits.

Children from such homes often physically abuse their wives and children and are repeatedly angry whenever frustrated. When this learning process takes place early in a child's life, and it is intense, you can be certain that those habits are almost poured into concrete.

Why are they called crazy?

Our understanding of craziness, or insanity as we professionals are want to call it, changes in time and place. In some societies you're insane if you say you're getting messages from God over your TV set; in others you're considered a saint if you have a vision of the Virgin Mary.

Early in my career I worked as the chief psychologist of a state mental hospital. In that capacity I saw practically every form of extremely disturbed behaviour. They fitted the stereotype of what insane people were supposed to act like. They spoke unintelligibly and had delusions of grandeur. That's what we have always thought of as insanity.

That still largely holds true today. But the word 'crazy' has been enlarged somewhat by popular usage to include behaviours which are highly irrational, if not downright outlandish. For this reason, we loosely use the term 'crazy' to mean actions which are out of sync with commonsense. Be that as it may, it's a handy term when it describes highly annoying people, even if they're otherwise bright, employed, married, sociable, but yet very difficult to get on with.

So that you don't think I'm referring to these populations in a totally exaggerated form, let me show you why I regard such terms as fairly justified. For example, if the behaviours of these crazy-makers can easily be found in any psychiatric textbook, would that make it easier for you to view them as deranged? If not, then what would? As you'll soon learn, four of the crazymakers I'll describe in the pages ahead are clearly persons requiring mental health services. They aren't actually insane or crazy, but you tend to feel like that the longer you know them.

The results

Exactly what happens to you when you live or work around a crazymaker depends on how well you can cope with their difficult behaviours on the one hand, and which difficult persons you're dealing with on the other. It obviously makes a difference whether you're dealing with a bully who abuses you physically or emotion-ally, and living with a loving parent who spoils their brats.

Among the worst consequences of dealing with the bullies are fear, dread, guilt, depression, low self-esteem and anger. These are only some of the more common emotional results of living with violent and angry people. Physically, you can sustain very serious injury and may be hospitalized.

If you live or work with a control freak, however, you'll first lose your confidence. Then you'll let yourself be dictated to until you become despondent. Rather than stand up to these dictators, you'll learn to keep your mouth shut. The usual emotional discomfort will come from depression, fear and anger. Self-blame – for cowardice from tolerating turning over your life to the control of others – will cause guilt and inferiority feelings, both of which combine to develop depression.

Should you live or work with a brat on the other hand, you could end up furious, fall out of love, feel drained, taken advantage of, and then be accused of being selfish. You'll lose some sense of judgement because your beliefs as to what is correct and moral will be challenged by these demanding and whingeing cry-babies. Again, you'll become depressed, usually from feelings of guilt, and you'll become tense or anxious for fear you'll be rejected. To avoid those consequences you'll cater to the brats in your life, but to no avail. No matter how much you do for these sweethearts, it's never enough: they're bottomless pits of demands.

And then there are the losers. These are poor, pathetic souls who are so negligent of themselves that those who love them and want to relieve them of their suffering end up pulling out their hair at the hopelessness they experience at trying to be helpful. Losers suffer from a modified death wish or an actual death wish. A huge belief in their own worthlessness which deserves all the suffering they can manage to generate flies blatantly in the face of their loved ones, who are doing their best to get them to act in self-interested ways. The conflict between the losers and the enablers can be maddening.

I could go on and on through the numerous types who frustrate us greatly, but I don't think it's necessary. Surely you get the idea by now how irritating and exasperating crazymakers are to their victims.

Now what about the physical results of crazymakers? Though psychological pressures on victims are always part of the crazy-maker picture, physical abuse is also part of that picture, some of the time from control freaks, but more frequently from bullies.

These persons are almost always males, whether they be boys, adolescents or adults. Testosterone – the male hormone – is largely a male characteristic. When women are violent, they're usually the brats, the spoiled ones who aren't getting the loving attention they demand, who can be life-threatening. When scorned they act like violent men.

Let's focus on the men. They are clearly in the majority of the bullies. Their victims are frequently beaten, intimidated, and even murdered. They have few or no feelings of guilt, they have the firm conviction that people who frustrate them are bad and that the best way to change bad people into good people is to be extremely severe with them.

Aside from the psychological and physical pains these people perpetuate on their families and employees, there are the tremendous stresses this causes marriages and jobs of the victims. A normal person who hasn't been thoroughly coached in the methods of emotional control as taught by rational emotive behavioural therapy (REBT) can't be expected to cope as effectively with this particular brand of crazymaker as those who practise REBT.

I am referring here particularly to the bullies and the control freaks. The former use force a large percentage of the time. Control freaks, on the other hand, use force sparingly, and even then their force is confined to less violent methods than are used by the bullies.

Other crazymakers I'll describe in this book are simply difficult to get along with in a variety of ways. Though they're not life-threatening, they're demanding, threatening, use emotional black-mail, and in general are so irritating that they're enough to drive you to a therapist's office.

Finally, let's not forget the sad effects of crazymakers on children. It doesn't take a genius to appreciate the negative consequences on children who live in a home where parents fight and scream. Terror, distrust, helplessness, guilt and feelings of inferiority are almost always present in some combination when living under these conditions.

These are the potential candidates for mental hospitals years later because of the unpredictability of their youth. These are the children who as adolescents or young adults might end up in prison. This shouldn't surprise us since violence and disregard for the minimum standards of decency teaches children to solve their problems with anger and hate. It always dismays me that the abusive behaviour of adults is so readily adopted by the children who themselves have been treated abusively. How do we account for this? Why would people repeat behaviour on others which they themselves went through and dreaded? The answer is simple: they were taught it.

You may not like the sound of the language you speak but if it's the only language you know it's clearly the language you will have to use.

In the same vein, children who see parents drink, smoke, swear, steal and cheat are dangerously prone to imitate what they see and hear. How can they do what they were never taught? Thus, we're left with the sad realization that many adult abusers were abused children.

Coping with crazymakers

I'll discuss four subjects which are helpful in dealing with disturbed people. In this section I won't be specific and explain which methods should be applied to a particular crazymaker. Instead, I want to show you that you're not as helpless as you might imagine, and that literally dozens of strategies can be employed in dealing with these frustrators.

Physical methods of protection

These obviously apply to bullies, sometimes to control freaks, less often to brats, losers and slobs. The best physical protection we can all develop is our strength. If you're small and/or female, this suggestion is especially appropriate to you. Granted you're no great threat to a 16-year-old adolescent who weighs 195 pounds (14 stone). But you have an even chance against someone in your weight and height class. Simply put, the stronger you are, the more you are able to defend yourself against others who are weaker. Join an athletic club, a gym, and build stamina. It'll do wonders for your confidence. When you move yourself up on the pecking order, life simply becomes more pleasant.

If you don't want to join a health club, then get into a weekly exercise programme that gives you 30 aerobic points a week. The guide I went by was Dr Kenneth H. Cooper's book *The New Aerobics*. It taught me that if I wanted to be aerobically fit I had to exercise four times a week and jog 20 minutes. In cold weather I jump on my trampoline instead of running outdoors. Then I do 30 pushups, 30 stomach crunches, 50 deep-knee squats, a couple of back exercises, and end up with another 30 pushups. This last group of exercises (after the jogging) only takes five minutes. As a result of this short programme four times a week I am able to play a vigorous one to two hours of tennis, bike 50 to 60 miles, and ski all day.

Be that as it may, I still wouldn't enter the ring with an experienced and more powerful opponent. But I wouldn't hesitate to stand up for myself in a dispute simply because I have less fear of being physically dominated. (Some women have saved themselves from danger because they were strong enough to fight off their attacker or they were swift enough to out-run him.)

Aside from physical strength and speed I also recommend men and women get instruction in the martial arts. Take boxing or karate lessons. Being able to inflict pain on to an attacker is very comforting in overcoming the fear of being powerless.

Finally, buying good locks for your home, installing burglar-proof systems and memorizing police phone numbers can all bring more peace of mind.

Social methods of protection

The lesson to be learned is: be careful what you wish for, you might just get it. Too often we're too trusting. We fall in love with people who turn out to be our worst nightmares. Therefore, always try not to let your love blind you about a relationship which your friends or family can easily tell you is going to be a disaster. In addition to enjoying the charm and politeness of your lover, always ask yourself what negative qualities your heart-throb also has. In short, be somewhat sceptical.

If you feel tense or anxious in a relationship you're probably better off delaying your decision to get married or cancelling such plans no matter how close the wedding date is.

Furthermore, it is always wise not to quarrel with people who are known to be highly temperamental, especially if they are under the influence of alcohol or drugs.

Financial methods of protection

Never minimize the benefits money can provide in safety against bullies. It permits victims to get training in self-defence, martial arts and guard dogs. With enough money you can build walls around your property or even have guards patrolling the grounds. The well-to-do all over the world have used those strategies for years, and to good advantage. Regrettably, they're limited to the wealthy. But you don't have to be rich to leave your present employment if it's threatening you. Find a new job first and then quit your present one. By the same token, if your neighbourhood is being overrun by undesirable people, money can help you move to a safer environment. Best of all, with enough money you have the ability to leave your abusive family or mate. Money not only gets you instant respect, it gets you safety and peace with the mere writing of a few cheques that pay for moving expenses and the deposit on another residence.

This is why I also caution all women to save enough money so that they can pack up the kids at a moment's notice and safely spend a night in a bedsit. Even having a couple of £20 notes hidden in the car, purse, or shoes have come in very handy to some of my clients who needed to leave home quickly when the man of the house turned into a bully.

One of the best advantages of having enough money is the ease with which legal help is obtained. Restraining orders, legal separations or divorce papers are readily available if you have the money for a solicitor.

Let's never minimize the blessings of money. It can generate more mental health all by itself than hours of counselling. Money does not bring happiness, but it can bring much comfort and safety. That's all we often need.

Legal methods of protection

Never ignore the power of the law. Even without funds you can still get the police to protect you from the bullies. However, after they arrive be sure to press charges for his arrest. Don't back down the moment he cools off and the police are speaking with him. Not to carry out your plan is equivalent to rewarding his. The behaviour you tolerate is the behaviour you encourage. If you don't press charges after the police arrive your abuser will realize he's called your bluff and, surprise, surprise, he has nothing to fear.

It is high time that society, especially the victims of abuse, act politically and have laws passed to protect women and children from these sinister and highly disturbed people. This has already started, whereby anti-stalking laws are being considered. Though the task seems difficult, take courage in the knowledge that many of our most compassionate laws began life being discussed by a few persons gathered in someone's front room, and ended up being passed in Parliament.

Psychological methods of protection

This is a subject I am most familiar with. The recommendations I've given above have limited application for protecting yourself. It will surely not have escaped you that not everyone can be strong, fast or fearless. Many people will never be able to defend themselves against bullies or control freaks. They may have no choice but to live lives of great frustration and semi-slavery.

Psychological protection is available to practically all lay people. People have a thirst for knowledge about themselves, especially how they think. This is where I can be the most helpful.

Therapeutic theories called cognitive-behavioural therapy (CBT) are available to us all. A special school of CBT called rational emotive behavioural therapy (REBT), mentioned previously, is the one I'm very familiar with. I won't elaborate on REBT at this time, but will explain its techniques as they apply to the particular crazymakers I'll discuss in the coming chapters.

As you study my views try to relate them to yourself and those you live and work with. Learn how these people become human headaches and what works best in dealing with them. You won't get magical solutions, I regret; nothing is that easy. But I'll give you psychological techniques and insights that will ease your frustrations, even if you won't always be able to remove them totally. In this way your life will be easier, you may help crazymakers to grow up, and you'll hopefully detect the crazy elements in your own behaviour.

2

Control freaks

The name I've given this particular group of characters gives their traits away. If you're one of them, what I'm about to tell you will seem very familiar.

First of all, you need to run the show; everything has to go your way. If you're not leading the band you're miserable, as though you have to make all the decisions. When you make a statement everybody must agree with it. To have people give opinions different from your own is a threat.

Dynamics

What makes you feel this way? It's because you want to feel superior. You believe that leaders are better than followers. Giving orders rather than taking orders makes you stronger, more intelligent and a better human being than those who take orders. Furthermore, you have very low frustration tolerance, you get bored and annoyed when you have to put yourself out for others. But you work like a beaver for anything that will benefit you.

In other words, you're power hungry, not necessarily through physical force but through economic and political power. Being rich is very important to you because you think that people who have more money are better than those who are poor. And you love having political power because then you can order masses of people around, not just a few in your own home. That's why military leaders are often control freaks. Rulers of all types, throughout history: kings, emperors or sultans have all sought power through being rulers because they could have the world exactly as they wanted it. They're people who seldom spoil others, but they practically always spoil themselves. No wonder that people want to be control freaks.

If you can't be rich, you might be an unethical lawmaker or judge and pass unjust sentences determined by prejudice or bribery.

On a more gentle note we can see the same thing happening in classrooms. If you're a teacher you have great control over the class.

For example, you choose who speaks and who doesn't. You tell every child in the room where he or she will sit. The homework is assigned by you, exactly which chapters and how many pages must be studied, and what kind of written work must be done. These are all dictated by you, the teacher. I had a Latin teacher once who had no qualms whatever in assigning homework which took three hours to complete. When we were quizzed on our material the next day it only took a few mistakes for us to end up with poor grades. That woman was a control freak.

Some control freaks browbeat their victims after they themselves have been mistreated. For example, suppose you're the low man on the ladder at work: you do everyone's bidding, you're bowing and scraping to everyone and it's 'Yes, sir' and 'No, sir' all day long. You reach a point, I'm sure, when you're wondering if you could control others for a change. And of course you do. When you get home you can get tough with the dog, the baby, the children or your partner. You control anyone just to get some balance in your life.

I once knew a scout leader who had no authority over anyone during the day in his job, but he was a no-nonsense person when the troop met each week. He could throw his weight around and get everyone lined up, give orders to his staff and see to it that the troop worked according to his fashion. And he loved it!

Different types of control freaks

The paranoid type

Control freaks exist in all degrees of intensity, from the mild to the disturbed. Paranoid control freaks can sometimes be menacing and highly frustrating. For example, they might insist that the whole family throw away certain foods which they are convinced are harmful; or they might insist that the TV be shut off because it was emitting dangerous propaganda. It wouldn't matter whether the rest of the family rejected the notion or not – to a paranoid control freak it becomes an extremely important issue and he would simply insist upon having his way.

The obsessive-compulsive type

If you are this type of control freak you'll generally be very concerned with keeping things in order, to a perfectionistic degree. You'll be preoccupied with controlling what people think and say, even in your most intimate relationships. By the time you're a young adult you probably will have developed at least four of the following:

You tend to be extremely concerned with making rules, lists and details to such degree that you forget why you're doing the whole thing in the first place.

You're a perfectionist to the degree that you can't finish what you're doing. One of my clients, a PhD student in literature, was writing a thesis on an aspect of the early 19th-century writers. When he reached the third chapter he couldn't go any further because it didn't suit him. Instead of finishing it the best he could and going on to other chapters which he might have been more comfortable with, he just couldn't budge from that stalemate and go on. His perfectionism was so intense that he believed if he couldn't do it exquisitely he shouldn't do it at all.

You're work-oriented. You want to produce, to achieve, and you're not at all interested in having a good time or smelling the roses. Leisure activities and friendships are simply not terribly important to you. You stick your nose in your bank account and fuss over every penny you can't account for. You split hairs, and thus reduce your efficiency.

Because you're a perfectionist, you will naturally be overly conscientious. There will be no leeway in your value system. What's right is right and what's wrong is wrong, and the two shall never mix. When you encounter others who have different moral values, you tend to be intolerant.

Since you're so determined to do things perfectly at all times, you can't turn over assignments to others or delegate work to others because they might not do it 'the way it should be done'. Only when you're certain that others will follow your advice precisely will you let them continue, but not without your supervision.

Having those characteristics will tend to make you very rigid and stubborn; another cardinal characteristic of this type of control freak.

Along with this goes the tendency to hoard, to be tight with money or with possessions. Being a penny-pincher, it's very difficult for you to throw away things which are worn out or worthless, even if they have no particular sentimental value.

You will perhaps have identified people in your life who would be diagnosed as obsessive-compulsive control freaks. You probably have some of them at your work place. These men and women make great middle managers because they can be ruthless. Some are slave drivers; they care only about numbers, about how much people turn out, about being on time, about making sure they put in a day's work for a day's pay.

Their rigidity forbids them to let up once in a while, even when nothing would go wrong or affect them seriously if they did back off from their sternness. What matters to them are the orders, the lists and the job.

That is the incredible feature about the obsessive-compulsive control freak: they don't see the forest for the trees. Such a mother or father will be very rigid about making sure their children take music lessons, and be so rigid with the process that the children end up hating music. It doesn't seem to occur to them that if they back off a bit and give them a break occasionally, make it pleasurable and fun, they would be much further ahead. No, for them an hour of practice is 60 minutes, and if it's five days a week, it's five days a week. Never mind if you're tired, never mind if you have a friend over, never mind if you're not feeling well, you paid for the lessons, therefore, you must put in that time every day at the same time for an hour, and nothing less will do.

If you're having to cope with one of these control freaks and you're ready to pull your hair out because you're sick and tired of always having to comply with their orders – be patient. I will devote a section toward the end of this chapter to that very subject.

The deluded type

A delusion is a belief which is so unrealistic that it can't usually be taken seriously. There are five types of such disorders:

- When you believe someone famous or from the upper-crust of society is in love with you.
- When you believe you're special, powerful, very bright or are closely involved with a famous person.
- When you feel you're being treated unfairly or threateningly, and that people are scheming to hurt and slander you.
- When you falsely believe that you or someone else has a physical defect or illness.

The jealous type

This is a delusion I will elaborate on as it is common and can be very distressing for all concerned.

17

Robert and Sue

During their eight months of dating Robert showed himself to be a warm and caring partner. He had a good job as a supervisor in a manufacturing company, and appeared to have a comfortable lifestyle after his divorce from his second wife three years previously. He was presentable, courteous, a pleasingly good-looking fellow with a small circle of friends. In short, Sue thought she had as good a husband as she could have expected.

It wasn't until about three months into the marriage that Robert began to make gentle complaints about her friendliness with his male friends. He thought a married woman would look more dignified if she shook hands with men, not hugged them. She thought this odd but didn't protest: no more hugging or kissing other men, despite the fact that she thought it was somewhat cute and flattering. But he was jealous at her cosiness with men, so Sue obliged him simply to silence his insecurity.

Big mistake. In the following months he became bolder, insisting that she never wear a dress which revealed her cleavage. She wasn't permitted to dance with anyone but him, nor answer the phone because it might be a man trying to get friendly.

Being a new bride, Sue didn't quite know what to do about this. Somewhat conservative in her upbringing, she was taught that the man was the head of the home, what he said went, and that making waves this early in her marriage was a sign of immaturity. Besides, Robert was so nice to her when she gave in that she learned not to protest too much.

It was then that Robert showed his true colours. He didn't want her to answer the door, even when she knew her parents were expected. When out walking, she was to keep her eyes cast downward so as not to attract the attention of passing men. At work she wasn't allowed to mingle with men, and when her duties brought them together she was ordered to do it with dispatch and in an unsmiling manner.

It got worse. If she was tardy coming home, even by five minutes, she had to account for the time. Letters to her friends or family were censored by Robert lest she report unfavourable comments about him.

Sounds unbelievable? Take my word for it, I've heard this and similar accounts of jealous men and women that would make your hair stand on end. Sue was clearly showing the wear and tear of living with this severe control freak. When she came to me she had lost weight, was depressed, harboured intense resentment which she kept completely to herself, and lost all sex drive. This was an irritation Robert couldn't tolerate: if she wasn't getting sex from him, she had to be getting it from someone else. The pressure and questioning he forced on her from then on were the type police give their suspects. Of course, Sue could never convince him she was faithful. His mind was made up, she had to be hiding the truth – maybe physical force would get her to confess.

It never did of course. Instead, Sue decided to leave Robert, especially after she took my advice and contacted his first two wives. Wouldn't you know it? They both had had similar experiences to hers.

Dynamics

What makes jealous people so jealous? Why can't they see that no one is usually after their partners? On the contrary, when the partners or lovers of jealous people get fed up with such highly disturbed behaviour, they don't want to run into the arms of another partner. No thanks! They're so tired of pleasing their partners that they want only to be left alone. After experiencing the nightmares with their partners as I've described, the last thing in the world most of these victims want is to start another intimate relationship.

But the jealous person can't believe this because he or she is completely convinced there is another lover involved, and nothing – or almost nothing – can weaken that belief. Why? Why can't these people believe they're loved by partners who want to be loyal? What is it which drives them to be so unsuitable that the one thing happens, by their own doing, which they dread: losing the love of their partners? The answer is that they suffer from a bad case of low self-esteem, or, to put it more simply, an inferiority complex.

The jealous control freaks make three characteristic errors in their dealings with their partners. First, they are so unsure of themselves that they always come out losing in a comparison between them and the other people the partners are engaged with. No matter who Sue related to, Robert would always be afraid she would enjoy them more than she would enjoy him.

The only way we can understand this need to compare himself

unfavourably with all her male contacts – with the possible exceptions of male children and aged parents – is to conclude that Robert had no faith in himself. Never mind that he didn't trust Sue, he also, and foremost, didn't trust himself.

So convinced was Robert of his inferiority as a lover that Sue's contact with practically any male was enough to send him into a jealous rage. He was sure he would lose her unless he stepped in and made her avoid all male contact. When she pulled away from him over this bewildering behaviour, he again couldn't see clearly that she was turned off by his ugly accusations – not because she found a dozen men she preferred over Robert.

The first error jealous control freaks usually make is to think 'I am inferior to practically anyone my partner talks to. My partner will surely make the same comparisons I do, me against the others, and I'll come out losing. I'm no good. I can't believe my partner loves me. I still don't know why he/she married me. What do I have to offer her/him compared to what others could offer?'

The second error the jealous control freaks commit is to conclude that if they're found to be inferior to others they will surely be rejected. The simple fact that they're still married after 30 years doesn't seem to sink in. If their partner's were so certain to leave them, then when is this horrible event to take place? If it hasn't happened in 5, 10 or 20 years, why should it happen tomorrow?

The truth of the matter comes down to this: their partners could fall madly in love with others, but how likely is that? Jealous people think it's absolutely going to happen every time the phone rings, or every time two people say hello. Nonsense! Most people intend to remain faithful unless they're driven crazy by control freaks who can't let well enough alone.

The third error jealous control freaks make is that they assume that if by chance their partners do fall in love with someone else, it will devastate them. First, let's agree that it's not entirely unlikely that their partners will reject them. After all, if they've been behaving like a typically difficult person, they certainly aren't acting like a sweetheart. They suspect correctly that their partners are not as crazy about them as they once were. That possibility not only exists, but it's increased the more difficult they become.

So, when they've pushed their partners away by their insane jealousy and get rejected, they should take it on the chin: they're getting what they deserve; they're getting what they worked for over weeks, months and, yes, even years. And of all things, now that they've achieved their goals they yet again falsely believe they can't live if they get rejected. I assure you their lives won't end because of the loss of a loved one; at most it will be very unpleasant, but still bearable.

Teenage control freaks

So far I've described control freaks who are adults. Now let me introduce you to the children, and especially the adolescents who grace our lives. They can be every bit as vexing as the adults. One such adolescent control freak is the oppositional and defiant type.

Along with being oppositional and defiant, these teenagers tend to be angry, negative and very difficult to get along with. If they've been this way for six months or more, and if they show at least four of the following behaviours, they're in this category.

- They easily lose their tempers.
- Their anger is often directed at adults, but especially their parents.
- Not only do these youngsters argue with parents, they openly refuse to comply with their rules.
- They enjoy annoying others. Maybe it's for the attention value, maybe it's to prove they're more powerful than adults. Whatever. They enjoy being pests.
- When they stir up a hornet's nest with their resistive behaviour and everyone is yelling at them, they turn around and blame their mistakes and defiant behaviour on others. They actually don't see how they could be responsible for all the yelling and cursing that's going on.
- When given orders, these teenage control freaks become very sensitive and annoyed. They become resentful and want to strike back at the authority figures who are giving the orders.

Judy

Everything in Judy's young life was going along smoothly, like a well-oiled machine. Her grades were high, a university scholarship was assured, she was attractive and she was 15. She was a darling to her parents. Then, out of the blue, Judy began showing signs of becoming a control freak. She defied her parents: this sweet, young thing turned into a witchy, defiant teenager right before their eyes. They could hardly believe what they were witnessing.

21

But that was just the beginning. The disagreements turned into arguments, which turned into yelling matches. Told to complete her homework, Judy would lie and fail. Told to clean her room, she insisted it was her room and she'd clean it up when she felt like it.

Some of Judy's friends were of questionable character. Her mother warned her about travelling with unsavoury company, but this only infuriated her all the more. Soon Judy was going with the people at school who had poor attendance records, poor grades, smoked and drank or took drugs, and even shoplifted. When a group of girls urged her to slip on a sweater in the fitting-room of a large shop and walk out with it under her coat, they were all caught by a suspicious security guard. The next day Judy was talking to me in my office.

The power struggle

There are usually four reasons why children misbehave: for attention, revenge, a fear of growing up and, lastly, to prove they're more powerful than their parents. Judy entered that time of life when she had to prove to herself and her parents that she had a mind of her own. This phase of growth is called 'the power struggle'.

If you've been through it yourself, or if you've experienced it in one of your children, you know what I'm referring to. It can happen before adolescence, but it doesn't happen to every child who wants to be more independent. Some can wait and are willing to put up with mum and dad telling them when to come home, to keep their rooms neat and to get a haircut.

Despite the fact that the power struggle can give you grey hairs, it has to be said that it has a healthy aspect to it, even if it is ill-timed: at least these kids aren't afraid of growing up.

Standing up to adults has to be done sometime in the young life of our children. They will almost never come into their own until they do take their stand, especially against the parents. Who wants their children, when adults, to be as obedient as they themselves were as children? Such people never grow up. Therefore, when we need to control defiant children we must be careful not to overdo it.

Coping with control freaks

To avoid having your life taken over by the troublemakers I've been describing – as well as others who want to control you for different reasons – you will have to apply certain techniques to all of them, and sometimes specific techniques for particular controllers. To be most helpful, I'll explain how others learn from you what they can get away with, and what you can do to get them to change. Obviously, not everyone who frustrates you will change, no matter what you do. In most cases you still have choices which can bring you relief. Let's start with the three principles of human interaction.

The first principle states that we get the behaviour we tolerate. The obsessive-compulsive control freak doesn't treat everyone he meets by insisting on having his way. He may try this approach at first, but give it up if he gets too much resistance. Whenever he does succeed in being demanding, he learns to repeat the pattern with that particular person.

Therefore, if your partner or parents, for example, are running your life, recall the first principle of human interaction and realize that you probably taught them to do this to you. How did you teach them to control you? By letting them get their way when they did it. You rewarded their behaviour, and that made it stronger. When a mother tells her children to come in for supper and they don't end their play, she'd better be very careful what she does from that moment on. If she has to call them two or three times, she'll have taught them not to mind her until her voice sounds loud and angry. They didn't obey quickly because they learned from past experience that if they continue to stay outdoors they can get another 10 minutes before mother loses her patience.

Remember that the greatest share of our behaviours are learned. Don't think that demanding people such as the obsessive-compulsive, or the delusional jealous types, or oppositional children got that way because of their genes. Modern research indicates that about 50 per cent of our behaviours are learned. And where and how do control freaks learn to be so difficult? From the people they live and work with, that's where.

I've worked with, and we have all known, adults who have temper tantrums when their demands are not met. The resemblance they have to whingeing and angry cry-babies is remarkable. Therefore, to deal with immature adults we have to use methods similar to those we used with our children. We have to go to the second principle of human interaction: others will not change until we change first. After all, they behaved badly towards us because we permitted it. It

23

follows, does it not, that before they will change their behaviours, we must change ours?

The third principle asks the questions, 'What do we change?' The answer is: our excessive passivity. And just how are we supposed to do that? By following the three rules of assertion.

Assertion

Just what is assertion? It's nothing more nor less than this: when you stand up for your rights *without* anger you're being assertive; when you stand up for your rights *with* anger you're being aggressive. Unless you're being attacked physically, I don't recommend aggression. It usually leads to violence and war. Relationships do not prosper when one party is the master and the other slave. Partnerships or jobs which are subject to repeated acts of anger and abuse are always unhappy and get worse, not better.

Assertion is a method you can use all the time with crazymakers. Granted, it won't always work – nothing does. However, your likelihood of getting some of the changes you desire are definitely increased when you become more assertive and less aggressive.

Cooperation, respect and love

In the final analysis, the conditions we seek from others are cooperation, respect and love. They differ one from another in the degree of sacrifice we expect from those we deal with.

The least amount of inconvenience we ask for is from simple cooperation. If our arms are full of groceries we hope someone won't mind opening the door as we leave the shop. We expect civil treatment because we are barely imposing on others.

Respect calls for sacrifice. When we tell someone a secret we hope he will respect our wishes enough to keep it. If we lend our car to a friend we trust, he or she will not take shameful advantage of our offer by putting on a few hundred miles until it's returned. Though the temptation might be great to abuse the favour, out of respect for our wishes we expect our property to be treated with care and not abuse.

Love calls for the greatest sacrifice. From those we love we expect loyalty, to be put first before all others. All earnings are to be shared with us, not others. A lifetime of favours is done for us, not others. Even one's life is expected to be sacrificed, so great are the expectations from love. If a woman gives her partner one of her

24

kidneys, we can be certain she loves him and wouldn't for a moment do that for just anyone.

Three rules of assertion

To attain these behaviours in our dealings with people we need to follow three rules.

First, if someone does a good thing for you, do a good thing for them. In this way we reward desirable behaviour, making it more likely to be repeated. Positive reinforcement is a scientifically proven method for training animals and children. There's no reason to exempt adults.

Second, if people do something bad to you and don't realize they've behaved badly, reason with them once. Explain why you're displeased and how you want them to change. If the undesirable behaviour occurs again, reason with them again. Don't get angry. Turn the other cheek. Go the extra mile and forgive seventy-times-seven, as it says in the Bible. That is the second and hopefully last time I advise you to use reasoning as a way of removing frustrations. You have been showing loving behaviour by being patient and understanding.

But suppose they do the unkind action a third time? Whatever you do, don't repeat your verbal complaint. You must now realize that the person is obviously immature or disturbed and won't listen to reason. To repeat your complaints many times teaches them not to take you seriously. Instead of words, you must now use actions.

Third, if others do a bad thing to you a third time, and reasoning has not helped, do something equally annoying to them. But it must be done without anger, guilt, pity, fear of rejection, fear of physical harm or fear of financial harm.

Until you can control these six emotions you won't be an assertive person. For instance, if you get angry with control freaks, you give them the right to use anger also. The inevitable result is conflict. If you experience guilt when you get tough you're likely to back down and give in to those you want to change.

The manager of a machine shop suspended a young worker for tardiness, then felt so badly about what the loss of income would do to the young man's family that he apologized to him for being so tough and let the matter pass with only another warning. Needless to say, the young employee quickly changed his estimate of how much he was hurting his chances of being dismissed.

As with guilt, the same happens when we back down for reasons of pity. The mother who wants to teach her rude daughter to show more respect by forbidding her attending a school dance, may feel so sorry for the child as she leaves the room, a tear in her eye, a sob in her voice, and shoulders hunched in defeat, that the mother can't carry out her threat, and decides to give the girl a lecture and one more chance.

If you have a problem with rejection, then again you will find it very difficult to be firm. Amy wanted to teach her husband to pick up after himself, especially his wet towels, pants and socks. It made her feel like his maid. He, however, when criticized, would distance himself from her for days. He would be polite but very cool, and that was what she dreaded. Until she was able to learn through counselling that she had every right to expect respect from him, and that he wasn't upsetting her greatly by being so aloof, did she manage to endure his rejection. She held out longer than he did, and eventually they spoke about the issue of his helping out more around the home.

Thus far I've focused on the first four conditions: anger, guilt, pity and fear of rejection. They're the easiest to control and the ones you least have to back away from using. The last two conditions: physical harm and financial harm are different.

When we're confronted with mean and vicious people who will hurt us unless we do as they say, the best thing to do is to give in. The same applies to financial harm for obvious reasons. Very often we let control freaks have their way because we fear for our physical and/or financial safety. That's why the boss usually gets his way, and why a woman doesn't quarrel with a drunken husband. The best defence we have is to avoid dangerous people on the one hand, and, on the other, to make enough money so that we're not dependent on others for our welfare.

Specific recommendations

When dealing with an obsessive-compulsive type, be prepared for a battle. If your frustrator is anyone other than an authority figure (employer, police or bully), you'd better begin your training of how to deal with those people as soon as you realize they're controllers. Don't wait too long before you protest or else they'll get used to giving you orders.

A woman saw me for counselling once who complained of her husband's dictatorial manner. She was aware of his bossy ways while dating, but tolerated them. This gave him the message that she was the passive type, precisely what he was looking for. Naturally, he didn't change after marriage. Quite the contrary; he was encouraged to come on as strong as he liked.

After you have reasoned with your strong-willed frustrators once or twice, say no more and make a plan as to how you will respond the next time they become intolerably domineering. If they are habitually late, keep them waiting, also every time they repeat that thoughtless act. If they're rude at a party, warn them you will take your own car and leave them at the party if they do anything improper.

If such tactics don't work, increase your pressure to make them more uncomfortable. If that doesn't work, you may need to increase your negative behaviour a notch each time the frustrator does. If nothing seems to help, try another penalty – or give up and tolerate the situation without resentment. If you get tired of that, maybe you'll get relief if you separate from the relationship for a few days to a few weeks.

These are highly recommended strategies when dealing with compulsive bullies. Be careful, however, as things will get very stormy in most cases. This is the price you will have to pay for breaking the old habits of control freaks.

Separations in a marriage can be achieved in four ways:

- Withdraw your intimacy and live with your partner as brother or sister.
- Leave the home voluntarily for some days, weeks or months.
- Get a legal separation. (If married, this assures you of all the financial protection you had under the marriage contract.)
- Divorce.

Coping with jealousy

Coping techniques with jealous people vary depending on how disturbed they are. In the most severe cases, separation or divorce are usually all that is left to you – unless of course you can tolerate the slave-like conditions you will have to endure.

Hopefully, the highly insecure control freak will be willing to enter counselling. Though major improvement is not likely, it's worth a try. That leaves medication as a last resort, which may help reduce the delusions of suspicion.

As far as less-disturbed jealous controllers are concerned, professional counselling can be of help, but your handling of their behaviour can also have a significant impact. For instance, you might point out to your jealous partner that everyone is inferior in some way: who, after all, is so perfect that no one outshines them? The burden they put upon themselves to be the best looking, best lover, best dresser and most humorous is simply incapable of being met.

You can also assure your partner that meeting pleasant people seldom leads to separation or divorce. Jealous people, like all of us, meet desirable people weekly, but we don't automatically leave our partners. And the proof is the fact that you and your jealous partner are still together.

Lastly, you can remind them that even if they are rejected, it hurts only as much as they make of it. As much as they may desire love, they hardly need it now that they're adults. Children need love; adults don't. We adults certainly want love, but can do without it quite well for months or years if we lose our partners.

Strategies for coping

Now a few words for you, the victim of a jealous partner. These are a few of the best strategies you can use to help them to change.

First, don't put up with their questioning. When asked why you are ten minutes late, give one or two answers. People who care for each other have legitimate concerns as to the welfare of those they love. If the questions continue, however, I urge you to refuse to answer because it will only reward further questioning. Jealous people won't take kindly to this behaviour, granted. However, it is still the best course of action, since whatever you do will be uncomfortable. Not responding may bring forth anger, but it increases the probability of extinguishing the behaviour. Responding gives you immediate relief, but strengthens the habit.

Second, don't change your behaviour to suit the demands of jealous people. Remember always that jealousy is their problem, not yours. *You* don't make them jealous, *they* do. So why should you change? Would you take an aspirin for someone else's headache?

True, if you didn't show attention to others, jealous partners would relax. But is that going to bring you happiness? Relationships thrive only when *both* partners are able to satisfy their deepest desires and needs. And remember, they need you more than you need them – assuming you're not equally as jealous.

Coping with teenage control freaks

To deal with control freaks who are your own children, you must know about the power struggle. Youngsters often tire of taking orders from parents. Most of the time they go along with our rules and give us no back-talk. Every so often, however, especially during early adolescence, a degree of defiance is shown which isn't typical of our sweet and happy sons and daughters. In the space of two weeks the most agreeable 14-year-old can turn into a difficult and defiant monster. Thus we have the power struggle.

What these children are trying to prove is that they're more powerful than the adults. Parents and teachers, however, are convinced *they* are the more powerful: they're bigger, stronger, wiser and have more money, so naturally believe they're bound to win any contest with a small, dependent boy or girl.

So, who *is* the more powerful? The children. Why? Because they're indifferent to the consequences of their actions. They don't care if they do poorly in school. University is years away. Being undisciplined is much more fun. Order them to study and they'll daydream out the window. Warn them about the bad influences they'll pick up from the unsavoury friends they associate with, and they'll see them at school. They'll smoke when out of sight of their homes, and in general fight you in a dozen ways in order to prove you aren't as powerful as they, and you might as well admit it. Ignorance of the future prevents them from seeing the dangers awaiting them; they couldn't care less.

Do we let them lie, steal, argue and defy us? Of course not! But we can't always make them behave sensibly by persuading them of the problems they'll soon have to deal with. Instead, we admit to them we can't make them act smartly, and if they insist on acting stupidly we won't protest. Instead, we'll let them suffer the consequences of their actions. They asked for it.

If they refuse to bring homework home, allow them to fail their classes. Perhaps, if they have to repeat them and we don't harp on how they caused their own problem, they'll think it through calmly and begin to take life and school seriously.

They leave on the lights when going to school? We unscrew the bulb, dismantle the lamp and lay the whole thing on the bed. And we never say a word.

A child won't keep the seatbelt secured while the car is moving. We pull the car on to the shoulder and wait. When the belt is connected again, without a word being said, the car moves into the traffic.

See how it works? Instead of trying to force them to do our bidding, we don't fight it. Instead, we let them make their judgements and learn to live with them. If they don't like the choices they're making, they can always do things our way. It's a great deal less stressful.

3

The bullies

This is the meanest group of crazymakers of all those I shall be discussing. Not only are they mean, they can be downright dangerous. These people scream their heads off, break property, throw dishes and slam doors, with or without provocation. They live by the rules of the jungle. All of you who are reading this and can identify yourselves as bullies would do well to take stock of your behaviour and your attitudes. Your kind of behaviour is among the most undesirable displayed by human beings.

Bullies think they run the world. Simply because they can intimidate most of the people they encounter, they readily use their physical advantage to get what they want.

You may wonder why I haven't included these people in the chapter on control freaks. There's one essential difference between the two. Control freaks simply want to control. They can use charm, clever strategies, salesmanship, or whatever; but they're content to get their way without violence if possible. Bullies, on the other hand, insist upon having their way, and they don't care what they have to do to get it. As you shall see in the next section, the major difficulty these people have is in controlling their anger.

Dynamics

Bullies have short fuses. They don't make a clear distinction between what they *want* and what they think they *need*. For them, wanting something is the same as needing it. It isn't unusual, for example, for a father of a family to want his children to do well in school and come home with decent grades. One bully, however, felt personally slighted and humiliated, as though it were a reflection of him when his son came home with a low grade in mathematics. To make sure that his son raised his grades in the future, he proceeded to harangue and intimidate the boy.

The findings of research into physical abuse by men against women make two recommendations: first, don't let your abusive partner return once you've made the separation; second, get out of the relationship if you can, and make it for good. Don't listen to endless promises of reform and to the tears shed while making these promises. Until you've seen realistic growth toward maturity, especially after intensive and lengthy counselling, don't even consider continuing with the relationship. We want changes, not promises.

Women are also capable of physical abuse against their partners and children. However, men, because they are physically stronger, tend to use force as a means of solving their problems much more readily than women, who have to use their wits or diplomatic charm to avoid people getting angry with them.

Physical violence has been used as a method of solving human problems since mankind appeared on the face of the earth. All you have to do is read a detailed history of the world and you will quickly learn that countries and kingdoms fought against each other with amazing regularity for centuries.

One of the ugliest characteristics of bullies is that they're simply self-centred: they couldn't care less what your problems are; they don't care whether you're hurting, whether you're innocent, or have a good reason for your actions. When they feel like letting off steam, they do so because it gets rid of their anger. Unfortunately, this doesn't always work. More often than not the anger increases – bullies may become more violent when they let go of their anger.

Anatomy of anger

To truly understand bullies you have to understand their psychology. I'll give examples from my book *Overcoming Frustration and Anger*, and also refer you to a book by Terry London, *Managing Anger*.

Basically, anger starts from wanting something. If you don't get what you want, you may then change your mind and believe you should or must have what you first thought you wanted – you convert your wishes into demands. If your demands aren't satisfied, you become angry. Then you think the person who's frustrated you is bad because bad behaviour makes bad people. Lastly, you believe that one of the best ways to make them into good people is to be severe with them.

There are four serious errors in the description which I just gave you.

First, no one makes you angry but you. If other people actually made you angry, then every time they frustrated you, you would have to get just as mad. Obviously, there are days when you're furious over a piece of stupid behaviour which you manage to ignore the next day. The only way to explain this inconsistency is by realizing that one day you talked yourself into anger and the other day you didn't. This applies to every occasion when you become angry. You talk yourself into your anger, unless something physical goes wrong with your brain: other people are not responsible for your emotions, and you're not responsible for theirs.

Second, you don't have to have everything you want. Stop changing your sensible and reasonable wishes into neurotic and unhealthy demands. You're not a child. The world wasn't made just for you, and just because you're right doesn't mean you have to have your way. Stop and think what others use as justification for their behaviour. They think they're perfectly right too. So why should they give in to you? You're both using the same argument. Instead, remind yourself that it would be good if you got your way, it would be preferable to do so, surely, but just because you want something doesn't mean you have to have it.

Third, people who behave badly are not bad. There are no bad people in the world, just bad behaviour. You can't judge someone on the basis of one or two, or even a dozen, acts of behaviour chosen out of a lifetime.

Correspondingly, there are no good people, just good behaviour. However, once bullies convince themselves that someone is an evil or annoying human being, they feel justified in cursing and intimidating him or her unmercifully.

Lastly, the thought that we can make people better if they're treated harshly is utter nonsense. You bullies need only stop and think about why you have your problems in the first place, and you'll see my point. Practically all of you people at one time were treated in severe ways. You were led to believe by your mothers, fathers or guardians that you were always upsetting them, that you were worthless because of that, and to teach you a good lesson, they would give you a good whipping. That was supposed to make you a wonderful human being. Instead, they taught you to be violent. Yet you're using the same methods you were raised with, despite the fact that you hated them when they were used on you. Can't you see that you're not doing anyone any good by using these same methods?

All adults automatically regress to the level of a child whenever they're angry. I'm sure you've seen children with tantrums, and that they get into that condition because they didn't get what they thought they needed. However, when anger happens in the case of children it's understandable because they're only children.

Stop and think what you're doing when you become angry and furious. Aren't you becoming a child and having a temper-tantrum just like an infant does? True, you're not getting all upset over a sweet, because that's not you're thing. But if you don't get a pay rise, or if you don't receive sexual gratification when you want it, or if somebody steps in front of you while you're waiting in a queue, you act like a baby and think that these people can't do that. Because you made a demand out of your wish, you're having a temper-tantrum. Your fit isn't any different than a child's fit, other than the fact that the child's was the result of not getting an ice cream, while yours was because someone broke a promise.

Different types of bullies

Let's start off with the category that first describes children who behave like bullies, and then I'll give you the categories of adults.

Teenage bullies

This group is typified by children under the age of 18 who have a pattern of behaviour which ignores the rights of other people. A person will have three or more of the following characteristics during the past year, and at least one of them during the past six months to describe him or her as a bully:

1 Shows a distinct tendency to be aggressive to people and animals by bullying, threatening and intimidating them.
2 Starts fights and resorts to weapons which cause serious harm.
3 Is cruel to people and animals, and has stolen belongings by mugging, purse snatching, extortion and armed robbery.
4 Frequently forces victims into sexual activities.

The second group of symptoms refers to the destruction of property, for instance:

5 Sets fires with the intention of deliberately doing serious damage, or tries to destroy property without setting a fire.

The third large category has to do with stealing and deceitfulness.

6 Breaks into homes, or often lies in order to get favours, and 'cons' others. Steals things of significant value but without confronting the victim, such as by shoplifting or forgery.
7 Violates serious rules such as staying out late against parents' permission. Starting at the age of 13.
8 Runs away from home overnight at least twice while living with parents, or runs away once but does not stay away for a long time, or truants from school. Beginning at the age of 13.

Antisocial types

This group includes those who are 18 years of age and older.
An antisocial personality will show the following characteristics:

1 Disregards the rules of society and is arrested fairly often.
2 Is a liar, uses false names, and cheats people out of their property or money.

If you recognize yourself by these characteristics, impulsivity is one of your greatest problems, and it interferes with being able to make plans. You get an impulse and you act upon it as though you don't care what happens to yourself afterwards. But you are often the one who is bothered the most when you are arrested or fined, something you could have easily anticipated if you had taken a moment and used your head sooner. You are aggressive, easily irritated, and you tend to solve most of your problems by fighting. You are also a reckless person and you don't care for your own safety or the safety of others. You are often a poor employee because you are so irresponsible. You can't be depended upon, and when you make financial agreements with others you have a tendency to betray promises. Lastly, you don't seem to care how much you mistreat others.

Occasionally explosive types

In this category are people who may be very nice a good deal of the time but who every so often lose control and strike out with amazing force, in a response that is out of proportion to the perceived injury. People in this group are unpredictable and may use force in a very mean and destructive way. They may falsely believe that:

- somebody has upset them;
- they have to have their own way;
- people who don't give them their way are bad; and
- if they are very very tough with them they will change bad people into good people.

An individual can change every one of these items if they believe the opposite and they will be surprised at how calmly and maturely they will eventually learn to react to life.

Breaking the anger habit

There are two ways for all of us to break habits. The first is through self-help techniques: books, audiotapes and/or videotapes. Or, second, you can go into individual or group therapy. Either way I would expect you to understand a few very simple but crucial pieces of insight to help you over your hostilities.

The first is that no one upsets you but yourself: you talk yourself into becoming furious with others. If you don't believe me, just ask yourself why everybody in the world isn't a bully since we all suffer frustrations, but we certainly don't all act like we're ready to drop an atom bomb on the world.

A second insight to help you break your bullying habits is to realize that your approach to problems doesn't set up a kind of society or world that people want to live in – and that includes you as well.

Realize also that making people afraid of you doesn't make you superior to them. You don't become better as a person because everyone steps off the pavement when you come along. If you think you get love and respect that way, you're sorely mistaken. People respect you when they fear you mildly. Anything greater than that simply creates outright fear.

Another piece of good advice for anyone, but especially bullies, is to think about the consequences of their behaviour. Bullies have low-frustration tolerance and are their own worst enemies because they don't care how their behaviour will eventually hurt *them*. You're the one who determines whether you will be divorced from one partner after the other; you're the one who gets yourself fired from jobs because you start fights or speak rudely and break things.

A little forethought would teach you to be more careful about what your actions are going to earn you. When you act like a wild ape, expect to pay the consequences. The cost of such behaviour to you is infinitely worse than putting up with the frustration you're using to justify your anger.

Decide instead to grow up, be civil, control your impulses and have respect for others. You don't have to express every one of your angry feelings. In fact, you hardly ever have to be angry at all if you watch yourself carefully.

Coping strategies for the victims

If we're ever to get control of the bullies we must get over the notion that these people must be loved and understood, and that this in itself will help them to behave better. Unfortunately, that isn't the case. A simple analysis of what is happening in the world today with our youth will tell you immediately that children who are not even teenagers, and the teenage group itself, are often incredibly disrespectful of adults and of the law and have no fear of the consequences of their actions. True, many of them have been raised by brutalizing parents or guardians. Probably their aggressive ways would never have taken root had they been treated with more understanding and patience when they were younger. However, we can't take those gentle techniques which might have worked when they were toddlers and apply them to young adults. For this reason we must return to former ways to deal with this problem today.

This doesn't mean that we need to hit our children, or scream at them and tell them how worthless they are. All those behaviours make them worse. When we use great meanness and hatred towards them the natural response we get in return is hatred. In fact, their anger against us becomes justified because we used the same methods. So why shouldn't they? What we need instead is to be firm and yet kind. That is a healthy combination of behaviours which can work wonders with people. To do that, most of you readers who have problems with bullies will have to overcome several psychological problems or your coping with them won't work.

The first is that you must not deal with these people by being angry. As I've pointed out, anger begets anger. We don't want to have a war on our hands. When we're dealing with angry people we want their cooperation, not their hostility. Chances are they can be

37

meaner to us than we can ever be to them. So let's not use anger. Let us instead use firmness, and take that as far as necessary in order to correct their behaviour.

For those who commit the kind of offences that all of us deal with week in and week out in our families and at the workplace, the penalty needs to be a moderate degree of discomfort. If we make people uncomfortable with their negative behaviours, but start off gently and gradually to build up the discomfort to a point where it hurts, they may feel more inclined to change. Let's not discuss and argue with them endlessly to justify our penalties. We want to advise them once or twice what we expect from them, and when that doesn't work, we get tough. That's called tough love. It means we'll make them sufficiently uncomfortable time after time until they change. Then if they don't change, we either accept them as they are or we break off the relationship.

One adolescent who I counselled was so angry that he took his hostility out on his younger siblings and even on his parents. The father was a gentle soul who couldn't stand up to his tall, 14-stone, 16-year-old son. As a result the youngster had his way at home. I urged the parents to penalize him and take his car away when he acted improperly. They agreed. The first time they did, the boy trashed the house. It was such a violent scene that they realized the boy simply wouldn't obey and that they had no power to make him do so. So they backed off and put up with his aggression. Unfortunately, they had tolerated his rude and inconsiderate behaviour for years, and by the time they decided to get tough, it was too late.

To refresh your memory let me review the three principles of human interaction which explain why people treat us the way they do.

The first is: you get the behaviour you tolerate. Ultimately, we teach people to do to us what they do. This means that this family, by letting the boy get away with rudeness taught him to be foul-mouthed and inconsiderate. He got his way and was rewarded for his aggression. When we reward aggression we get more aggression.

The second principle states: others won't change until you change your own behaviour first. This is what they attempted to do by becoming totally intolerant of his rudeness and taking his car away. They were right to do so.

The third principle is: Reduce your excessive toleration.

The psychology of respect

Respect is a tricky word. It has three meanings: appreciation, admiration and fear. If I tell you that I appreciate my mother and father for all the sacrifices they made throughout my life, you will surely understand what I mean. I respect them, I love them, and I am eternally grateful for all they did for me. But respect in that instance is synonymous with appreciation.

If I tell you I admire the incredible feats achieved by the space programme which sent a man to the moon and that I have enormous respect for all the people involved in that whole programme, you will again easily understand what I mean. I'm not referring now to appreciation for what they've done, but rather to the sheer wonder of it all.

The third definition of respect is mild fear. If you want respect from people you must make them somewhat afraid of you. Mild fear, at the very least, is what is necessary to make our children respect us. They'd better learn to fear us, the police, the teachers and the authorities in society. If they don't fear us they will not respect us.

I would even go so far as to say that if one adult does not fear another adult mildly the two can't fall in love successfully. Love comes from respect, and respect comes from mild fear. You cannot love an adult who you're not mildly afraid of. If you don't fear the person you're relating to, you will do whatever you like. You'll think less of that person for not stopping you from your inconsiderate behaviour. You'll treat that individual as though he or she were a servant of yours, not a lover or an intimate person. I say again, if you want others to love you, make them fear you, not greatly, but mildly.

The same applies to parents. You can't get children to obey you until they fear you mildly. They will then be afraid to behave badly. By behaving acceptably, you will treat them more kindly and lovingly. Then you will be rewarding good behaviour by giving affection. None of this would have happened had you not made your love conditional: 'Satisfy my deepest desires and needs and I'll satisfy yours. Refuse me and I'll make you uncomfortable. My love must be earned.' That's the dynamic behind fear leading to love.

Having explained these principles let me now apply them to single mothers who have rebellious adolescent children.

Single mothers need to understand that they will be practically powerless to raise their adolescent children properly unless they use sufficient power over those youngsters when they are children. If the children have a healthy degree of respect (mild fear) for their mother then she can give her 16- or 17-year-old sons or daughters orders which will be obeyed. If she doesn't have control by respect she will be defied, and this happens more easily today because present societies tolerate rebelliousness. During adolescence children may want to smoke, drink, stay out late, go with whomever they like, and follow their own desires. They often have no idea how dangerously they are behaving and no amount of reasoning gets them to see this. Therefore, a mother in such a predicament needs to use force since words don't work. But whom can she rely upon? If she doesn't have a husband then she ought to call on a grandfather, or perhaps the children's uncle. If they are not available, she still needs to find an authoritative male who can come in and put some mild fear into these children if they disobey.

A second change we need in our society is to make the children fear and respect the law.

It is always best if justice is meted out swiftly. I have personally worked with any number of adolescents who did not hesitate to commit one offence after another though they were arrested shortly after their misbehaviours. It took weeks or months before they appeared before a judge. Eventually a fine or a penalty was placed. The process is so slow and the penalties so mild the children learn not to take the law seriously.

Make the justice swift and make it fit the crime. Whatever you do, stop talking about the problem. If there is one mistake I notice people make more often than any other when dealing with people, it's that they repeat themselves endlessly over their complaints. Make your complaints on one or two separate occasions. Then do something about it.

The psychology of conversations

There are two kinds of conversations. The first is a discussion and the second is an argument or a quarrel. A discussion takes place when two people are simply exchanging information, gossip, jokes or directions. These are not emotionally charged discussions. One person is giving an opinion or information, the other is simply listening.

As the discussion continues, it's likely to hit upon a subject or statement with which one listener doesn't agree. You, for example, will say that your friend didn't deserve to lose his job. The person you're talking to says he was a bad employee and deserved everything he got. This is the kind of stuff which sometimes encourages fights. You will insist that you're right and that your partner is wrong. One or both of you will begin to raise your voices and insist upon getting agreement, and that the conversation will go no further until agreement has been made as to who's right and wrong!

Of course, that seldom happens. Usually voices rise higher, the table is pounded and insults are thrown. Before you know it, two people who were simply carrying on a discussion are now ready to fight. To avoid this scene, which, incidentally, seldom seems to change anyone's mind, follow these pointers.

First, realize that when you get angry you're not in the mood to listen to anyone else's reasoning. And the person you're talking to, who is also angry, is certainly not in the mood to listen to you. You've seldom won an argument just by getting furious. Also, the other person has seldom convinced you by yelling or threatening, and that you were wrong and he or she was right. So let's stop all this getting angry, because it simply doesn't work.

Second, the moment you notice that anger has entered into the conversation say 'anger'. That is an automatic signal for the two of you to shut up, turn on your heels and walk away from each other and stay away until you can talk yourself out of your anger. You do that by realizing the three incorrect assumptions we all make when getting angry: others made you angry; that makes them bad people; they should be punished in order to turn them into good people.

That may take you a while as you walk around the block. It may even take several days before you can get yourself calm. In any event, when that's been achieved it's time for you to get together and resume the conversation at the level of a discussion. If anger enters the conversation again, turn on your heels and quickly walk away to start dealing with your anger once again. Repeat as often as necessary.

This material on conversations is crucial because so many scenes of anger simply come out of the things people say. Yet words are harmless. You can't be upset by words. Get that through your heads. Sticks and stones can break your bones, but words can never hurt you. Remember that saying from childhood? Well, never were truer words spoken.

The psychology of assertion

Let us get over the idea that we want to give counselling to everybody who has an emotional problem. One of the reasons people break so many laws and give expression to their feelings so easily is that they are seldom penalized consistently and vigorously when they attack others. They know that society disapproves of their violence. Therefore, for us to sit them down and tell them again that it is wrong to take advantage of people physically is foolish. Why are we telling people something they have heard all their lives?

First we have to penalize them. There has to be a negative consequence and it has to be of enough potency to get people to change their minds. Bad habits change when people suffer significantly with a bad habit. How much does it take to make people uncomfortable enough to change? As much as it takes.

After it appears that the punishment has taken hold and these characters are beginning to think that maybe they would be better off in the future behaving legally, then let's offer them counselling. Until then they don't need talk, they need to be made increasingly uncomfortable. The suffering doesn't have to be brutal, it just has to be firm enough to get a specific result: respect for others.

Let me now introduce you to some ideas on how to handle people who are out of control. Be an assertive person rather than an aggressive one. I remind you from Chapter 2 that the distinction between the two is this: when you stand up for your rights without anger you are being assertive. I always recommend assertion over aggression.

I have seen any number of women who were abused by boyfriends or husbands. The men promised to change but never did. They would drink, stay home from work, live off the money the women earned, be unfaithful, and if caught, would glibly apologize for their misdeeds and promise never to do them again. I recently talked to a woman who left her husband on two separate occasions and he was truly contrite for being bossy and physical with her when he drank but he relapsed shortly after. My contention remained the same. She was still tolerating his behaviour.

Stop yelling at your partners and telling them what's wrong. They've heard those stories over and over. What you need to understand is that *you* have to change. *You* were too nice, nice to a fault. *You* gave in, and, instead of making people miserable with their dumb behaviour, you tolerated it.

How do you change and stop being so permissive? If you've spoken to the person who's frustrating you one or two times about what they're doing wrong, don't confront them with more complaints. If they haven't changed in that time, then reminding them a third or fourth or fifth time isn't going to help a great deal. Instead, do something equally annoying to them. But be careful that you don't do it with anger. If you do, you're going to have war on your hands rather than cooperation.

Second, don't do it with guilt feelings because, again, you're going to feel so badly about what you're doing that you're going to stop your assertive acts.

Third, don't do it with pity in your heart for the person who you're trying to make uncomfortable. The whole object is to do precisely that, to make the other person uncomfortable.

Fear of rejection is the fourth act you have to be careful of. If you fear rejection, you're not going to stand up to anybody vigorously. Rejection doesn't hurt unless you let it. You don't need to be loved to be a worthwhile person.

The fear of physical harm is of course a very legitimate one. If refusing to tolerate someone's mean behaviour is going to get you battered, by all means don't complain – escape as fast as you can.

The last condition to observe is the fear of financial pain. This is also a very legitimate one. Finances provide us with health and protection, a roof over our heads and bread on the table. To be destitute financially is literally life-threatening. If we're going to encounter physical or financial harm I suggest we *not* be very assertive. The price to pay for change may well be too great. Learn to tolerate it or get out of the relationship. Whatever you do, don't tolerate such relationships with anger. That's a formula for disaster.

What about love?

To deal sensibly with crazymakers you'll have noticed by now that you can't do it well if you feel hatred for them. However, does that mean we should love them unconditionally and thereby get them to stop being impossible? The answer is yes – but not in the way you think.

Most people think love is demonstrated best by the many kind and caring things we do for others. The common saying heard so often between lovers is: 'If you really loved me, you'd do me the favours I asked for.'

You see, love is viewed as the feeling we all get when someone gives us what we want, no matter how unimportant or how often we want it. The more we're satisfied, the more we love the person who does the satisfying. That's how I eventually decided to define love: love is that powerful feeling you have for someone or something who, or which, has, is, or will satisfy your deepest desires and needs.

This says in effect that we love people for what they do for us. Unconditional love makes sense only when we refer to children, pets or feeble parents. That being the case, how can we love crazymakers if love means their giving us everything we want? Wouldn't we be making them worse if we reinforced all of their immature ways? Of course we would. In fact, that's precisely how many of them became brats or control freaks in the first place. These people got what they wanted, when they wanted, and still they turned out badly. Doesn't this mean that unconditional love is wrong, harmful and neurotic?

The problem clears up nicely when we define what we mean by deep desires and needs. If we focus on satisfying most deep desires we could easily end up spoiling people. After all, deep desire usually means getting your way most of the time, having servants do all your chores, being able to play and enjoy yourself all day with amusements, food, drink and sex. If we treat our friends and loved ones in that fashion we do them a questionable service, and condition them to expect getting everything their hearts desire. Granted, they'll think we're wonderful people for being so generous. And they'll love us to pieces, but only as long as we're gratifying their endless demands. Deny them their wishes and watch out – that love can turn to hate in moments.

Now, let's look at the second part of the definition of love, the reference to needs. These must be distinguished from deep desires in that they're crucial to one's well-being, but aren't always desired.

To cure an infection, a child needs an antibiotic injection. But the youngster surely doesn't look forward to it. To make the most of his talents, a youngster needs to practise the piano and do homework nightly or he'll not live up to his potential and have the fulfilling life he's capable of.

Though the consequences are painful, they're crucial to the health and maturity of those who are treated so firmly. They might claim they are being treated meanly, but I would prefer to call it *tough love* if you will. They're not getting what they want; they're getting what they *need*. How can that be anything but a loving act? And it's these acts of love which crazymakers weren't shown. Either they were brutalized and not taught how to be gentle and understanding, or they were spoiled and given whatever they wanted while being denied the firmness and self-discipline they needed in order to mature.

We who have been treated with firmness along with kindness love our parents. We were made to behave in proper ways and to apply our efforts to bring out our best. My father saw to it that I practised the piano an hour a day even though I assured him I didn't like it any longer. In return he informed me how he held his father responsible for my father being a tool-and-die maker when he should have been a university law graduate. His father never made him study and attend college and he blamed his father for that neglect.

At the time my dad probably enjoyed the carefree life. As time went on, however, and he had to raise a family and could only do it on an immigrant's wage as a factory worker, did he miss having a higher education so that he could have learned a profession instead of a trade, and had life infinitely easier?

I assured him repeatedly that I wouldn't blame him if I decided years later that he should have forced me to play. His response was that I would blame him. Now that I've been an adult for 50 years and have enjoyed the piano in many moments of quiet, and now that I've lived as a professional person and had an interesting, challenging and fulfilling life, I know he was right and I would have blamed him. How pleased I am that he gave me what I needed (discipline), not what I wanted (to go out and play).

That is the difference that makes all the difference. Kindness with firmness works wonders, whereas kindness without firmness, or firmness without kindness, creates serious emotional complexes.

If we can agree that we must love our partners and family selectively, not unconditionally, then we must next ask:

To protest or not to protest?

When should we protest? When we're less than just reasonably content. Don't ask others if you should quit your job to protest unfair treatment on the job. Do it when tolerating abuse makes you less than barely satisfied. Use this same standard when you refuse to accept rudeness from your children or partners.

Use this standard when you think of breaking up a long friendship. What's right is to stand up for your benefits at a point where you feel you're still reasonably satisfied, not when you are below the JRC (Just Reasonably Content). If you suffer frustration after frustration in the belief that pleasing the other person will eventually be rewarded with considerate behaviour, you're likely to be sorely disappointed. Mature people feel obligated to reciprocate, to return kindness with kindness. Under those conditions making sacrifices makes sense. Often, however, when you give in to the wishes of others at the cost of denying yourself, and you don't get rewarded in turn, then make the assumption that the other party is immature and/or disturbed and is likely to take all the advantage of you that you permit.

Relationships work best when both parties feel content. When you pay too much for peace and make too many sacrifices which are not reciprocated, four conditions will occur.

The first consequence from not making yourself just reasonably content is that you will become increasingly unhappy. How could it be otherwise? We don't jump for joy when we're increasingly frustrated. The factory worker who doesn't get his pay rise after he's worked hard for the company beyond the call of duty, is sure to feel at least unhappy.

The second result of making excessive sacrifices for the approval of others is that we'll become disturbed. Such symptoms as depression, anger, anxiety or jealousy are sure to emerge. Being repeatedly frustrated is no fun; it's wearing and demoralizing and forms the soil in which disturbances grow.

The third consequence of tolerating abusive behaviour is that you'll gradually fall out of love. If love is the result of satisfying someone's deep desires and needs, the opposite of that creates loss of love. You rarely love people unconditionally unless you're a saint or a fool; hugging your partner after he or she comes home drunk is giving your partner a bonus.

Lastly, if love continues to diminish there's nothing left to nourish the relationship. You become distant, move out or divorce, pure and simple. If you can't divorce for religious reasons, separate. If you can't separate, the wish to leave will still be there. That is the final result of your living below a reasonable level of contentment.

4

The brats

We come now to another type of crazymaker who one would not normally perceive as such. These aren't violent, aggressive or dangerous people. Nor are they tinhorn dictators. Instead, these are the people who control others by acting helpless, by whingeing and being immature. They're the brats. These are the people who have been so pathetically spoiled that the only way they can get along in life is to have stronger people around to get their needs satisfied.

Brats are self-centred and deficient in compassion. They complain constantly and can't take no for an answer. Although they resemble control freaks in that they have to have their way, they don't usually get tough or abusive like the brutes. They cry, whimper, pout, beg or feel hurt. Guilt is liberally used to get all they want. To exhibit their pain, their lower lips stick out, their shoulders slump and they walk off to the privacy of their rooms hoping others will take notice and feel sorry for them. They're the takers of this world and their pit is bottomless. What you did today will not suffice for tomorrow: tomorrow you must repeat and do the same if not more than you did yesterday.

These adult children have levels of expectations which most normal people don't have. They believe they're entitled to the good life and that people should sacrifice for them. One of my clients told me about her father who could never accept being last in line. In a movie theatre he would simply go to the front of the queue, ask a question of the ticket clerk and then, while the question was being asked, he would throw down his money and ask for a couple of tickets. It did not bother him that he was cheating a dozen other people out of their rightful places to go before him. Brats only think of what makes them feel good – not what others are entitled to.

The histrionic brat

These people tend to be very emotional, want attention constantly and ordinarily are very demanding. They're uncomfortable when others are getting more attention than they are. For example, when a famous comedian was at a party and not getting most of the attention, he would immediately do some of his funny antics and perform a juggling act, just to be noticed. That's a major feature of the histrionic brat. Isn't that sad? How can an adult male be envious because others are getting more attention than he?

In order to be the centre of attention, some women brats use their sexual advantages to get the behaviour they want. When this doesn't work they may go from smiling, seducing and charming to being sarcastic. You must always remember that histrionic brats are immature emotionally, and their feelings go up and down just like a child's. To get the attention they want, they put special emphasis on their appearance so they can all the more easily lure others to their way of thinking. And when they speak in gushy and sweet terms, full of sentiment and feeling, they rarely go into appropriate detail.

When frustrated, they become models of dramatization. They act like strickened and distraught actresses who are undergoing the pains of hell. With the back of the hand to the forehead they are the swooners of yesterday, as they stomp their little feet and exit in a flurry of indignation.

Because of this emphasis on beauty and attention, histrionic brats naturally think that every effort paid to them is a sign of someone's enduring love. Not for a moment would they think that someone is only doing them a favour. No, the person is mad about them and an obvious love affair is about to take place, best describes their perceptions.

For most therapists, histrionics are headaches. They see them as adults who act like babies. They've been spoilt by well-meaning parents who have given in to their rantings and ravings until they can no longer appreciate the fact that there are others in the world who have rights, not just them.

Narcissistic brats

As though histrionic brats weren't enough, we also have the sad situation of the narcissists. These are people who not only have all the flavour of the histrionic, but also have a sense of grandiosity, a desire to be admired and thought of as highly special and entitled.

These brats have an exaggerated sense of self-importance. They see their own achievements as splendid and that they are full of talents which nobody else can match. They fully expect to be recognized for all their special abilities and their high achievements, and yet they seldom demonstrate that they've earned that recognition.

Narcissists are in love with themselves. That's where the name comes from. Narcissus was a young man in Greek mythology who fell in love with his own reflection when he first saw it in a stream. They love their beauty, talents, and just about everything else, and these are all regarded by them as better than anyone else's. Obviously, they see themselves as unique and special people who can only be appreciated and understood by other special people, especially those who are themselves gifted and who come from the higher levels of society.

Narcissists are very exploitative, they take advantage of others, they don't care about others and don't feel for them. They're often envious of others and believe others are envious of them. Of course, they have feelings of superiority, haughtiness and vanity. In short, these are annoying behaviours which make them difficult people to like.

The dependent brat

It's fairly easy to determine whether or not the person who is frustrating you so much is a dependent brat: simply check his or her characteristics against the following description.

These people generally have great difficulty making decisions and usually require a great deal of advice and reassurance from others that they're making sound judgements. Being dependent, they're naturally fearful of assuming responsibility for the important areas of their lives. Therefore, they welcome the opportunity for others to assume responsibility for them. Others will decide where they live, what they will wear, or what they'll buy.

If you're a dependent brat, you're certainly not going to disagree vigorously with others since you're so afraid of losing their approval and love. Rejection is proof to you of your inferiority, and the certainty others will also find you undesirable.

Naturally, as a dependent person you won't engage in projects on your own because you lack the confidence or ability, not because you lack any desire to achieve.

You will go to great lengths to get nourishment and emotional support from others, even to the point of agreeing to do things which are quite unpleasant to you.

You will feel uncomfortable a good deal of the time when you're by yourself since you're convinced you have no ability to manage life on your own. You want another relationship as a source of comfort and support whenever one relationship ends. Lastly, like any insecure individual, you're very concerned with the possibility of being left to take care of yourself.

It's no great difficulty to imagine what life with a dependent brat is like. One woman reported to me how her fiancé was extremely demanding and difficult to live with because he could do practically nothing on his own. His mother had spoilt him since childhood and he was still living with her now that he was middle-aged. The mother had no compunctions about bringing him breakfast in bed, cutting his meat, bringing his coffee to whichever room he was in, and helping him out financially whenever he was in need.

The man was incapable of independent thought and, therefore, pressured his girlfriend to assume all the risks of making decisions. Yet he seldom hesitated to show his strong disapproval of her when she acted unwisely. He insisted she take charge regardless, which she always did.

Because he was so dependent upon his mother, he would not interfere in the slightest with the normal difficulties that his fiancée and his mother might sometimes get into. To have confronted the older woman would've been a serious threat to his financial and emotional well-being, and he knew where his bread was buttered, so he favoured his mother over the younger woman.

Another dependent person comes to mind. Some years ago after giving a speech, an elderly couple approached me afterward to ask what they should do about a daughter who was constantly calling them for financial assistance. These people had recently retired and were financially comfortable. They soon were barraged by their adult daughter for money to help her over one crisis after the other. At first the girl wanted only £100 or so. Within months, she was crying on the phone, pleading that her parents give her £1,000. They asked me what they should do. I, of course, told them not to provide such funds since the girl was educated in schools of higher education and had a job. It was high time she learned to handle her funds better. This would never have happened if they had not rewarded her bad spending habits. I never heard from them again after that evening. Hopefully, they took a firm stand, turned the girl down and let her suffer the discomfort of her self-indulgence.

Does this necessarily mean that we shouldn't become dependent upon others at all? Certainly not. People are interdependent – with the possible exception of hermits who live deep in the woods, dress in furs and eat wild berries. The rest of us are dependent upon someone to sell us petrol, to give us work and to provide roofs over our heads.

Even more, there are times when all of us need a loving and generous hand to carry us through. One young man who recently obtained his university degree wasn't yet financially well positioned and wanted a loan from his parents so that he could have a down-payment for his house. I thought this was quite appropriate considering the financial status of the parents. Without that generous expression he would have had to rent for a long time before he could afford a down-payment. That was an example of a healthy degree of dependency. They knew full well that their son was hard-working, would be responsible and that he could be helped along in life much more quickly if he were given this boost to get his first home.

There are times when emergencies strike. Perhaps a young adult needs the services of a solicitor, or a doctor but is unable to afford them. Then the assistance of loyal family members or friends can come to the aid of these people.

These aren't dependent brats simply because they're receiving handouts and loans. These are mature adults who never would have taken this solution if it hadn't been absolutely necessary for them. They weren't being spoiled. These rare requests for help weren't common to them. That's the major difference between people who are dependent and those who are independent.

For the brat

The best thing you brats can do is give serious thought to the whole notion that somehow you're special and are entitled to privileges and favours the rest of mankind is not entitled to. Whoever said you're better than others? Why should you have the right to barge in front of a long queue of people waiting to get into a theatre or a restaurant? What makes you so different that rules which apply to everyone else don't apply to you? Do yourself and all those you associate with a big favour and talk yourself out of the belief that there are special people in the world and they deserve better treatment than others. And especially that you happen to be one of them.

Instead, put yourself in the shoes of those people you tend to look down upon. How would you like to have someone monopolize the conversation and never let you get a word in edgewise? Brats are notorious for taking charge of all conversations, talking about themselves at all times, and after a few minutes, or even an hour, of chatting with someone they come away knowing practically nothing about the person they've been talking to. Their thoughts are almost exclusively upon themselves, their lives and their experiences, as though whatever happened to the listener was insignificant: the trip he or she went on, their political views or stories are more important than whatever anyone else can discuss.

Try to realize that you're not the superior and highly esteemed people you delude yourselves into thinking you are. Your immaturity is so striking that others actually feel sorry for you when you think you're God's gift to the world because of your beauty, intelligence or wealth. The attention you so desperately seek is always going to be denied you in the long run because you can't be respected when you act like a spoiled child. You're a self-centred, whingeing complaining child, and I can assure you that you don't become popular or respected when you have these traits. You've never grown up. This isn't entirely your own fault. Your parents probably indulged you by giving in to your every whim. It's easy to do. Any child can be trained to be a brat: all you have to do is reward demanding and whingeing behaviour and you're going to have a first-class complainer as an adult.

I have on numerous occasions counselled such adult-children who were good-looking, strong, bright – but emotionally crippled and functioning at the level of teenagers. One fellow discovered, much to his surprise, that when he was a teenager he defied his father, who, instead of sitting down on the youngster, showed fear of him and didn't assert his parental authority. When my client sensed that his father was afraid of him, that was the end. From that day forward he did exactly as he wanted. He refused to do homework, refused to help around the house, spent money, caused mayhem in the home, went and came as he wanted, and in the process became a thoroughly spoiled brat.

My client thought he was on top of the world, but he began to learn fairly soon that nobody else thought well of him. His friends thought he was spoilt and tended to avoid him. When I saw him he was in his young 20s, he was very much alone, very much a failure in everything he tried, and bitterly complained that his father let him get by with rudeness and such little responsibility that those skills his friends learned in their teens he had to learn in his mid-20s, and do it all by himself.

A third skill you brats had better learn is not to rate yourselves. Maybe you're a fine athlete and you have a wonderful figure and you sing beautifully. Those things just make you more beautiful or talented. I compliment you for whatever achievements you have, but don't think for one moment that just because you're rich, handsome or skilful that you're better than someone else who doesn't have those qualities.

It isn't possible to rate an entire human being on the basis of one or a half-dozen or even 100 characteristics. There are literally millions upon millions of judgements that can be made about any one person. To take a few of the good ones and to say that 'Because I possess those, I'm better than you who don't possess them', ignores the fact that there are a multitude of things we could say about any person which are not being put into the equation.

People can't be rated as people. We can only make very detailed judgements about a person's characters or traits. We can only legitimately judge the finite, the extremely minute things about people, never the total person. 'He's a beautiful person', 'She's a wonderful woman', 'He's a great fellow', and other such statements are all unprovable. We must specify in what way a person is great, or intelligent or beautiful. I could say of my neighbour that he was a brave person last Thursday from 2:07 to 2:09 when he waded into a river to rescue a youngster from drowning. That doesn't mean he's always brave or that there aren't others who are much braver. All we know of my neighbour is that during that two-minute period, on that particular day, in that particular river, he acted in a brave way. It says nothing about how he would react today, or how he reacted in the past, or how he would act if he saw other people drowning.

Overcome the rating game, as I describe in my book by that name. The major flaw brats have is that you're always rating yourselves by how well you're dressed and how good you look, or by the fact that you have a certain skin colour or come from a certain family. You're

54

deluding yourself if you think for one moment that any of that makes you a better person.

For the victims

Unfortunately, those brats who read this aren't going to make all the lovely changes I've suggested. Therefore, those of you who live with them are best advised to make some changes yourself.

First of all, why do you tolerate such nonsense? As I mentioned previously: you get the behaviour you tolerate. Simply because these babies kick, scream and complain doesn't mean that they have to have their way. Give them a taste of their own medicine. Wail, scream and kick and show them that when they act up you can act up too. If you don't put up with nonsense you discourage nonsense.

The only reason people continue a behaviour is because we go along with it. We indirectly teach people how to do whatever it is they're doing. If we didn't reward behaviour it would stop. However, if it hasn't stopped, we can rest assured that we've played a very significant part, although indirectly, in the perpetuation of that situation.

Stop putting up with it. Give them a bad time. If someone does all the talking, force yourself into the conversation. Talk at the same time that others do whenever you feel they're monopolizing the conversation. Talk right over them and keep it up until they get the message. You're not going to be very popular with that person, but then who cares?

Whenever you try to change the deeply ingrained habits of others you're not going to win a popularity contest. Even though you may be doing them a favour in the long run, they're not going to see it. Expect to get rejected. The next time the group wants to dine out, make sure it's to a restaurant you like. If you're in the habit of letting a brat always watch his or her TV channel, get another TV and watch what you want; or simply take charge and switch to channels you prefer. In this manner you teach this poor creature the reciprocity law of social interaction. You can rest assured that these people weren't taught to reciprocate when they were youngsters. Their motto is, 'Gimme, gimme, gimme'. The idea that they'd better repay others for favours simply escapes them.

It's high time that you stopped tolerating living with people who have these faults. If you do the washing up one night, let them do it the next. If you often use your car for errands, let others take theirs next time. Make sure that you get fair treatment by not continuing the relationship if it's one-sided: stop it, end it, break it off until these brats see that they'll have no friends if they don't learn how to treat others with a fair degree of equality.

This means that we must now take the parental role and teach these children how to grow up. It doesn't matter if they're 50 years old, they can still be emotional children. But if we start treating them like adults who are expected to think of others, they'll become caring adults with high frustration tolerance.

If they resist all efforts to change, you may have to end the relationship. If so, end it. I've seen people become so tired, worn out and fed up with feeding these brats that they eventually divorced them. This also applies to the work place. If you can't get workers to reciprocate and to take their fair share of responsibility for the workload, get rid of them. If they're dismissed often enough they'll eventually wake up and begin to assume a more adult role. We get the behaviour we tolerate, and others aren't going to change until we change our excessively tolerant behaviour first.

But what if the person screams so hard you feel great guilt? Good point. It means that their emotional blackmail is working. The goal of emotional blackmail is to make you feel so afraid of the brat going crazy or committing suicide that you give in. If they can control you with emotional blackmail by threatening to become upset, depressed, to lose control and smash things and then blame everything on you, they win the day. But if you don't go along with them you'll soon notice significant changes in these immature people. However, you have to take control of three things which cause your cowardice.

First, don't feel guilty when you stand up to them. If you do, you'll back down and give in. But why shouldn't you feel guilty? After all, you're causing them considerable consternation: you're denying them things you probably could give into. It makes no difference. Don't feel guilty when you're deliberately trying to make someone grow up. Though they may think you're being very cruel, you must know in your heart that you're showing them a form of love that they've not had before. You're saying to your friend, 'I'm not going to go along with you on this. You owe me a favour in return and nothing is going to happen until you pay up.' Your friend may then get angry. So be it. Don't feel guilty: what you're doing is actually a very loving thing. It is showing love in one of the forms which these people probably had very little of: tough love, otherwise known as firmness.

A second coward-maker is other-pity. When you get tough with these people they're going to whine and cry and feel sorry for themselves. It may even be very genuine. However, that has nothing to do with the fact that they're still going to be spoilt if you give in to their whims and desires once more. If you really love them don't always give in to everything they want; instead, give them what's good for them. Denying them what they want can be the very best thing for them. You wouldn't give children all the sweets they wanted, knowing full well that they would get sick. You take the sweets away, the child hates you for a time, but you don't feel sorry for the child because he or she is having an emotional episode.

Remember, to feel excessively sorry and disturbed over other people's problems is neurotic. We care about people, we feel for them, we show compassion and we're our brother's keepers. However, that doesn't mean we have to suffer right along with them to the same degree they do. We're not helping people when we get so upset that we begin to become an emotional mess also. If you feel very sorry or heartbroken for them you're going to yield and then you will be perpetuating the same immature behaviour they've had all their lives.

The last coward-maker you have to be very careful of if you're going to work with brats is the fear of being rejected. Rejection is thought by some people to be the worst experience next to having their fingernails pulled out. Careful study of that whole issue shows quickly that you don't have to have the love and approval of everyone you happen to be involved with. Rejection doesn't hurt unless you make it hurt. If you think that you can't stand not being loved by someone, just ask yourself what you would do if that person died. Of course you can stand these things, and you can certainly stand to be disapproved of by your partner, your boss and your friends. You can stand to be rejected by all of them. You've been rejected before, probably dozens and dozens of times through-out your life, so why can't you accept this one as well?

I guarantee you that you're going to be rejected first rate when you don't give these emotional babies everything they want. Tolerate the rejection regardless. Show them they can't control you with their whingeing and crying. If they threaten suicide, tell them if they say it one more time you're going to call the ambulance and you're going to take them up to accident and emergency.

Call their bluff and don't go along with all their blackmail. They will use those tricks to get their way. They may sometimes feel that they're not blackmailing, that they really feel miserable enough to die. All the more reason for you to act as if they're that disturbed. I think some of these disturbed persons try to seek sympathy by walking out in the rain without a raincoat, burn themselves with cigarettes so that others will pity them and then give in to them, drink until they are drunk, all for the express purpose of getting pity. It makes no difference, these people are disturbed and if you think they're doing something which could hurt them badly, call the medics. If it isn't that bad, then let them suffer from their own manipulative behaviour until they realize that it's not going to get them anything.

When you control your guilt, your other-pity and your fear of being rejected, then you can be a truly loving person to these poor and badly trained individuals. They need help, they need friends and they need someone with a head on his or her shoulders, not someone who gives in to their rantings and ravings. That's precisely how these people got into such bad shape in the first place.

5

The losers

Here we have an oddity. It's hard to imagine that people make a habit out of making themselves miserable, but that's exactly what losers do. Some of them drink themselves to death, others end up in a hospital because they've ruined their lungs by smoking cigarettes for 30 years, and some never manage to diet well enough to keep their weight within healthy limits.

Let me give you typical examples of what these people are like. A man doesn't seem to accept advancement in his job. Though normally performing fairly satisfactorily, and eventually getting a rise and a promotion, he suddenly does so badly that it appears to his fellow workers that he engineered a problem so that he could be demoted or laid off. In this manner he has for years gone from one job to another, always starting off eagerly at a beginner's level, works his way up a bit until he begins to feel uncomfortable and then does something to sabotage his success.

This meant that he and his family had to move often, leaving town in the middle of the night with everything packed in the car because they couldn't pay the rent. When he got another job, they didn't hesitate to buy what they wanted, ate out whenever they wanted and eventually fell back in their rent payments and had to leave town again.

He was a charming fellow and could easily have made a good salesman. Instead, he used his charm to win favours from friends and family. Without great difficulty and with a tale of woe he could get his friends to open their homes to his wife and him for several weeks while they would try to locate a flat and get a job. They would use the telephone of their host; even long-distance calls for which they promised to pay, but never did. And they would help themselves to the food in the refrigerator, and make themselves perfectly at home, not realizing at all that they were wearing their welcome thin with their greed. In the end, in typically self-defeating fashion, they were eventually kicked out by their families and friends until they had nowhere to turn.

Yet, every once in awhile, he would meet new people at work or at a pub, turn on the charm and extract favours from these people with promises that he would repay them whenever he could get back on his feet. And the cycle would repeat itself. Occasionally, some of his friends who genuinely liked this couple would try to advise them. Their self-defeating lifestyle was certainly easy enough to see, but their friends and family couldn't understand why these people didn't learn from their negative behaviour.

Some of my clients who aren't self-defeating have reported frustrating experiences with people with this diagnosis. They would lend them money, cars, make phone calls for them, all for nothing. After wondering if something was wrong with themselves, the good samaritans would seek counselling. Whether they realized it or not, they had a crazymaker on their hands.

Another example was a gentleman who saw me because his wife was very depressed and morose and couldn't feel joy over anything. He was a hard-working man, sincere, and loved his wife dearly, but nothing he could do could make her happy for any length of time. The woman had a way of simply refusing to enjoy whatever good fortune he could bring her. She systematically damaged her health with drinking, smoking and erratic sleeping habits. His gifts to her were lost or damaged, as though she unconsciously couldn't accept being treated kindly. Eventually, the fact that she had a devoted husband must have been too much for her because she even jeopardized her marriage by having an affair, and did it in such a way that the husband had to find out about it.

The man was driven to distraction from not knowing what he could do to make his wife happy. It wasn't until I assured him that she didn't want to be happy and that she needed to have a good deal of counselling that he stopped blaming himself for her continued and unrelenting moodiness and reckless behaviour.

The symptoms

Self-defeating losers are people who simply avoid or sabotage whatever pleasurable experiences they might receive. They get into relationships and situations where everyone but they know that they'll suffer. When offered help they tend to turn it down as though preferring to suffer.

These individuals choose people to work with or to marry who will lead them into disappointment, failure and mistreatment, even when they clearly have other choices available. They refuse to let others help them, and either turn down such assistance or accept it but then manipulate events in such a way that it becomes totally ineffective.

When something good happens to losers, unlike other people who would respond with joy, they show signs of depression or guilt. Or they do something to themselves which causes them suffering, such as an accident, getting drunk, or breaking up a loving relationship.

They also instigate angry feelings in the people who are important to them, knowing full well that they'll be rejected. Yet when they are, they feel keenly hurt and humiliated by the experience. When they have a chance to experience the good life and could enjoy themselves they tend not to admit that they're happy.

Self-defeating losers may refuse or won't do the work that's necessary for them to achieve success despite the fact that they clearly have the ability to do so. They may help others at a skill and achieve advancement, but they won't do the same for themselves.

They remain uninterested and tend to reject people who are nice to them. Those people who can do them the most good are usually the ones they reject.

Their degree of self-punishment, which naturally brings on feelings of frustration and pain, is so steady and consistent that it clearly shows them as wanting to be miserable despite the fact that no one has asked them to put themselves out to such a degree that they should make sacrifices.

The causes of self-defeating behaviour

The primary psychological factor that causes people to be so self-defeating are feelings of guilt and inferiority. Somewhere and sometime in their lives they've been told repeatedly that they're inferior, will never amount to anything, and that they're disgusting and worthless people. These feelings of rejection are so intense that we must assume that the brainwashing which leads to this self-defeating behaviour was also intense and longstanding. They often come from homes where there's violence, screaming and yelling, great unhappiness, and people showing very little love. The effects this has upon the youngsters of such a family can only be imagined. Many children raised in homes where alcohol is abused and where one or both parents are alcoholics also fall into this category.

As a result of this negative brainwashing, these people learn to judge themselves as unworthy, undeserving and inferior. They're so convinced of being undesirable that when others find positive things to say about them, the losers find it to be so incompatible with their own negative views that they protest it. They'll try very hard to convince others that the nice things being said about them have to be false. If they're not believed, self-hating persons will do something to convince their friends that they're as worthless as they believe they are. To do otherwise would give them the feeling of being phonies and of lying to the world.

If they were to experience pleasure or accept a compliment, they would immediately fear that others would get the wrong idea about their being normal and decent people. Such an idea would have to be immediately erased by refusing to enjoy a positive experience or by sabotaging a good experience so that no one would ever get the idea that they're happy, good and decent people.

Guilt is a second powerful motivator of the self-defeaters. When they're told that they're worthless and have been treated like trash, they not only feel worthless, as I've just pointed out, but their feelings of guilt for trying to be otherwise can be so intense that they feel deceitful whenever they try to be happy and successful. Once they believe they're inferior but try to pass themselves off in society as good as anyone else, they know that they're lying to themselves and trying to fool others. Thus they feel guilty over that manipulation.

The whole act of guilt always says two things: First, that you've done something bad, and, second, that because you've behaved badly, you must think of yourself as a bad person. It's a two-pronged process. Simply doing something bad, ugly or cheap doesn't have to make you *feel* guilt for doing so. And they certainly don't become self-defeating losers as a result. We feel guilt only when we hate ourselves over our undesirable behaviours, not when we simply behave badly.

It is hopefully apparent now why losers are crazymakers. Those who fall in love with them, or who employ them or live around them can see as well as the loser that he is a self-punishing masochist. The need for them to make their lives miserable day after day escapes no one who knows them fairly well. And this of course brings out our feelings of help, love and compassion. These are pathetic individuals. Though often kind and gentle, they're masters at suffering who refuse the help of their friends and loved ones to stop the suffering.

And that's precisely why they tend to be so frustrating. We can go to great lengths to get them a job, which they then sabotage and are laid off from. We can buy them nice clothes, which they neglect. We can teach them a skill at great cost, which they refuse to master. Or we can present them with a car or a house so they can improve their standard of living, but they will in time then destroy the car through neglect or accidents and do the same with their homes. That's the crazymaking part of their behaviour. Try to imagine how frustrated and angry you might become when you see someone you care for slowly but surely destroying themselves despite all your efforts. You'll probably wind up depressed, angry and worried about what your loved ones or friends are doing to themselves.

Coping strategies for the self-defeating loser

The main problem losers have is that they're self-raters. They're in fact self-raters of the worst kind. Everybody judges themselves from time to time, but self-defeating people do it over practically any insignificant occasion in their lives. Therefore, one of the most important psychological skills they need to learn is never to rate themselves at all, for anything. And to do that they'd better understand that they can separate the rating of their behaviours from the ratings of themselves.

If you were to be praised for something you did very well you would have every right to feel proud and happy about receiving the praise. However, if you rated yourself as a superior human being to someone who didn't receive that praise or accomplish what you did, then you would be making the serious kind of mistakes I'm referring to. In that case you would be feeling conceited, thinking you're better than others. But suppose you had done worse than others? For instance, others received a promotion, but not you. If you were to conclude that you weren't as good as others as a human being, then you would easily feel guilty, inferior and depressed. Those emotional states practically always follow negative self-rating.

One of the most important tasks I advise you to learn for the rest of your life is that you cannot logically rate people. You can rate their looks, their intelligence, talent, character, wealth or values. However, it's just not rationally possible to rate a human being. You can only rate minor things *about* a person but not the whole person.

63

You can say that your friend is a marvellous dancer but you can't conclude that your friend is a marvellous person. You can't even say that your friend is always a marvellous dancer, only for a specific time. So your friend might have been a fine dancer during his or her adolescent years but is out of step with the modern dances and doesn't do much dancing today. The more detailed and precise the judgements we make about behaviours and traits the more accurate we are. The more sweeping and broad our judgements, the less accurate they are. The judgements which are global in nature, those about a whole human being, are never and can never be accurate at all. Why not? For the following reasons.

First, no one in his right mind would judge a human being by a single trait. That would be the same as saying that all people who are beautiful are superior and better than others who are ugly.

Second, you can't judge someone on several or even dozens of traits. Why not? Because even a dozen or a hundred traits would be a drop in the ocean compared to all the traits that you could rate a person by. If you want to rate people accurately you would have to rate them in every conceivable way both positively or negatively. You would have to add every positive judgement and subtract all the negative judgements and then determine if you came out with more positive than negative evaluations. If it were the former you could consider them superior persons. If it were the latter, you would have to consider them inferior.

That's clearly impossible. Just give it a moment's thought and you will realize that there are literally millions of good or bad things that we could say about any individual. Every good thing you ever did, every bad thing you ever did, every good or bad thought, every healthy and every unhealthy cell of your body, all add up as items for which you could be praised or faulted. Since they run into the millions there's clearly no way we could ever correctly describe a person no matter how many judgements we made since they would always be extremely few in number compared to all that could be made.

Another point to bear in mind is that even if we knew how many judgements we would have to make to rate a human being we would still have to agree on what makes a good or bad trait. Certainly not everyone in the world is going to agree that being a blonde is good or that having freckles is bad. Some would argue that having more than average weight is bad and others would say that it is a distinct mark of health and beauty. However, even if we could agree whether something is good or bad, the question still remains as to who would do the judging. Would it be all men or all women? Should they come from the west or from the east? Or how about some of them coming from Europe, Asia, South America and some from the United States? Widespread agreement on this would be highly unlikely. Even if we did we would then have to decide how many would be assigned to this group. Should it be a group of 10, 50 or 100? If you add or subtract even one person, the judgements about who and what is good or bad would change.

Another serious criticism about being able to rate people is the fact that you can't rate all characteristics as though they were equal. Being a beautiful person is one thing, but having a sterling moral character is another. I'm sure all mature people would say it's much more important to be honest, upright and responsible than just to be good-looking. However, how many more times is being a mature person worth than being beautiful? No one knows. It has never been studied. Also, for us to make the effort to compare every trait against every other one would be totally daunting.

The last criticism as to why you can't judge people is that even if all the objections I listed could be overcome, there's one that still stands in the way of making that possible: as time passes, people change.

It would take more than a lifetime to make one of these evaluations. In the intervening time the person has grown, matured, changed, sometimes for the better and sometimes for the worse. And that means that effort put into rating that person would be wasted.

If you understand this, you can never rate yourself or someone else again. You can never say that someone is better or worse than you as a human being. You can always say that somebody sings better than you or plays tennis worse than you, or is better looking than you, or is slower than you intellectually, but those are all individual and detailed ratings. They make sense. But you can never rationally say again that someone is a wonderful or terrible human being. Those are all global ratings which only focus on one or several characteristics by which we base our judgements while completely ignoring millions of other characteristics of that same individual.

Self-defeating people don't understand this. They take innocent events and use them to hurt themselves. These self-hating people have been brainwashed so thoroughly as children that they accept being inferior. Once they start believing this, they live up to that expectation. That's when the self-fulfilling prophecies of gloom and doom which are thrust upon them begin to take place.

If a young man is told he's nothing but a failure and is going to end up in the gutter, how can we expect such individuals to rise and shine, to grit their teeth and stick out their chests, face the storm and prove to the world that their parents are totally wrong? Quite the contrary takes place: they'll turn upon themselves. They will get themselves into trouble, lose their jobs, marry poorly, develop addictions, and often wind up in jail because it was predicted that they would be losers. They fulfil the role which was assigned to them. They don't appreciate or fully understand that they're simply going by a script which was given to them by their family. They don't question the idea that their parents might be wrong, and that even their brothers, sisters, friends or fellow workers can all be wrong. Men will wind up in jail, lead violent and destructive lives, women will wind up alcoholic, promiscuous, and badly married because they're fulfilling that silent directive from the voices of the past.

You losers to whom this is making sense take heart and realize that you've been brainwashed. Never mind that some of the things people said about you were true. Their conclusions nevertheless were false. In other words, when they said that you were slow, ugly or fat, that may have been the case. But they implied something else when they made those statements. They implied that, therefore, *you* were inferior. And that's precisely what you now have to challenge. Why aren't you an acceptable person even though you're out of shape, not smart or beautiful? Who are they to judge you or anyone else by one or two traits? We are all more complex than a handful of judgements. Human beings have infinite variety and have characteristics much more important and admirable than most people see.

Therefore, the major thing you have to learn is never to rate yourself badly. To be consistent, never rate yourself positively either. Frankly, however, it's less serious an error to feel superior than it is if you feel inferior. The inevitable consequences of putting yourself down are that you will have low self-esteem, treat yourself with disrespect and get depressed. And once you have achieved the status of a loser you will run your whole life in that direction.

Once you rate yourself as better than others you could easily feel strong, confident and happy. You'd be totally wrong, of course, because you'd be making judgements about yourself that could change overnight. Then you'd have to hate yourself. Don't do this. High self-esteem and self-love are both time-bombs ready to explode right in your face.

You self-raters and losers had better stop feeling guilty. When you rate something you've done and then you hate yourself for it, it's the hating part that does the damage. All of us make mistakes, millions of them throughout a lifetime, but we don't all develop serious neurotic problems. This is a technique you have never learned. Learn it now and stop believing every negative thing someone says about you. There are a whole string of things wrong with all of us.

Coping with self-defeaters

If you live with or work with a loser, protect yourself most of all by expecting them to do precisely that. They're losers, they're not going to enjoy life, they're not going to be happy when others are happy, and nothing you can do can generally make them very content. If they show signs of happiness and are getting ahead in life, and they are beginning to reach their goals, hold your breath because that run of good luck isn't going to last. Just when they could get ahead they will get drunk, swear at the boss, get a divorce, or do dumb things which will surely set them back to where they started. Remember, self-defeating people hate success. They're losers and must do whatever they can to keep themselves in those sick, neurotic ruts. If you understand that and expect it you won't be so disappointed. Instead, you will then calmly try to refer them to counselling. Of course, they'll probably refuse this because counselling is supposed to help people. Losers reject help like they reject praise. Quite the contrary, they don't want counselling, they don't want help. Then they'd have to enjoy life the way the rest of us do.

Helping losers

Be an amateur psychologist. Don't apologize for trying to 'psycho-analyse' people. The more you know about psychology and the better you can handle your own problems, the better off you are helping others. You can teach them what you've learned. Give your self-defeating partners and friends the best advice you can. And that's about all you can do for them. Be careful that you're not too helpful because you're only going to get hurt every time your best efforts are sabotaged. Therefore, don't give them money or your labours. Give them your advice and let them figure out how to achieve their goals with your advice. They're probably not going to take your advice, in which case they'll suffer again. If they want to ignore you that's perfectly acceptable. Sometimes they might be right and you might be wrong. We learn by trial and error. Mistakes are not terrible or awful, they're valuable stepping-stones to success.

If you're going to be an amateur psychologist, you need to become acquainted with the whole business of guilt and self-rating. Don't pity your self-defeating partner or friend. That often feeds the habit. Take it matter-of-factly, show proper respect and compassion for the jams they get themselves into, offer your help as long as it doesn't inconvenience you too greatly, and as long as it doesn't deny them the discomfort which should go along with their losing strategies. We won't criticize or yell at them, we'll simply let them suffer for their errors and be as friendly and gentle and as understanding as we can. We may even tell them that we're aware of their self-defeating needs again and that perhaps we thought they were over them.

What you don't want to do is have them drag you down so that you get depressed along with them. Don't become exasperated in the process of trying to help them. The more disturbed you are over their self-inflicted pains the more reward they get for having hurt themselves and the more pity they receive, thus the stronger that tendency becomes.

Remember always that they look to you as one source of punishment and unhappiness to satisfy their neurotic need to be miserable. If you marry such a person, and they frustrate you to the point where you hate them, yell at them, and want to leave them, that's the kind of food these self-defeating people live on. Going through those emotional whirlwinds simply feeds their neurosis because they're made all the more miserable by them.

Notice, what I have suggested is that you change yourself emotionally by learning a few important strategies which will help self-defeaters most of all. They don't need money or material favours in most instances; they need a change in attitude, which comes through a change in your attitude.

The martyr

A special category of losers are those poor souls who suffer from self-pity. This naturally leads to depression, which has the following symptoms: by feeling sorry for themselves, these victims of self-pity look for all the world like the classical martyrs of old. Like the Christians who were thrown to the lions in the Roman Coliseum, rather than give up their faith, the losers hold rigidly to their roles of long-suffering persons who want all the world to know just how much they have put up with injustice at the hands of an unfair world.

Family members who must deal with such self-suffering children or parents are made to feel totally frustrated because they can't seem to relieve the martyrs from their pain. This leaves the frustrated helpers feeling guilty and helpless. They try everything they can to help their loved ones, but nothing helps. 'What can I do for you, dear?' the martyrs are asked, but the answer is always the same: 'Nothing, I'm fine' is the answer. It's not true of course. The martyrs don't want the pain removed, for how could they justify feeling sorry for themselves? That's why they're so frustrating. We think they want relief; the truth is that they need to feel miserable either to gain the attention they long for, or they need their suffering to make others feel guilty for injustices they have committed.

Whichever it is, don't trouble yourself unduly over these self-pitiers. The more you fuss over them the more you reward their neurosis. They thrive on your worries, your tears, your pleadings. Instead, truly help them by doing the courageous thing, offer your help, give your advice and urge them to be kinder to themselves. Then let them do what they need to do. Put the monkey on their backs and show them that they, not others, are responsible for their miserable lives. It's hoped that when they get tired of being their own worst enemies they may give up their desire to blackmail the important people in their lives with emotional manipulations.

Harry

Harry was in his third year at university when he was caught cheating in an examination and was expelled. He moved back home, defeated, depressed. Others had also cheated in that exam but weren't detected. His parents and sisters naturally felt badly for him, and tried with all manner of gestures and kind acts to ease his pain.

In the past Harry always insisted all was well and that he was coming along just fine. But he would walk off with slumped shoulders and a sad and forlorn look and retire to his room where he would remain for hours. The family tried in vain to bring him out of his depression. No amount of cheering up had the slightest effect. In time his mother herself became depressed, thinking she had let her son down. Nothing she could do would ease his black mood, and her guilt intensified.

The family eventually learned to detach itself from his irritating moods. They accepted him as a neurotic and realized that martyrs must do what martyrs do. To expect Harry to be an optimist was equivalent to expecting alcoholics not to drink, brutes to be loving, and elephants to sing opera. Martyrs don't have to be martyrs all their lives. Change is possible, but not usually until they're shown how to change.

The family was able to detach themselves from his annoying personality by realizing that Harry wasn't picking only on them. His self-pity was a pattern he developed years ago and he used it whenever and with whoever he was dealing at the moment. I told his parents not to take Harry personally since, if we removed all of them from his life and gave him a whole new family, Harry would be treating his new parents precisely as he had his first family.

This brings me to an interesting realization about relationships which I made years ago. It explains why some disturbed people won't change, no matter how much pressure you apply to them. I know this is strange since commonsense would lead us to believe that stable people get their way more often than the unstable precisely because they're more practical, emotionally controlled and reason better. With all that going for them why or how in heaven's name do the neurotic members of a pair end up running the show?

Let's go back to the problems with Harry and his family. He was considerably more disturbed than his parents or siblings. Somehow, over the years, he had learned very poor habits. They barely prepared him for life as an adult. He avoided tough and unpleasant tasks, he had very low frustration tolerance, his insight was weak and left him with a false set of beliefs about how life truly works. He was unequipped for adulthood.

But his family were not. They all had high frustration tolerance.

They had fine control over their feelings and they were practical thinkers who usually thought about the consequences of their behaviours. They were the mature ones.

When Harry and anyone from his family disagreed, who do you think would bend the most to keep peace? Who was more capable of being objective and able to see a viewpoint different from his? The family of course. To avoid splintering the family and to keep it intact, the grown-ups were capable of putting up with some poor decisions if it meant Harry would be given more time in the hope he would eventually grow up. Therefore, they gave in to Harry because they wanted a united family.

In this case it didn't work. Harry continued to take advantage of the generosity and patience his parents showed him until they were so thoroughly fed up with his crazymaking that they helped him to get a semiskilled job, put him up in a small flat until he could assume monthly payments, and detached themselves from him therapeutically. They still loved their son but no longer expected him to change. It was easier for them to tolerate his weird behaviour than for him to grow up.

This situation often applies when we deal with bullies, control freaks, obsessive compulsives or even jealously delusional persons. If you find yourself in those relationships you may be dealing with persons so rigid, so inferior-feeling or so utterly uncontrolled that it will have to be you who changes if you want the relationship that badly. Counselling often doesn't touch this group. About the only thing that works is the pain they experience over the years from their crazy actions. When it really hurts, change is more likely to occur. But even then, don't bet on it.

6

Slobs, neatniks and pests

I gradually became aware over the years as I counselled many couples over their troubled marriages that a condition was causing them more difficulty and suffering than I would ever have suspected. I knew that many couples have financial worries, that they quarrel over sex, religion, rearing of the children, inlaws, work, socializing or just plain annoying habits. Anyone who is aware of the world at large knows people have big disagreements over those issues. One condition, however, also came up every so often which I wouldn't have expected being as serious as it apparently is. I'm referring to the war between the slobs and the neatniks.

There are millions of people who are casual about their dress, their homes and their appearance. Those men don't mind having a spot on their tie or that their shoes aren't brightly polished. There are millions of people, on the other hand, who dust their cars before going for a drive. They shower after mowing the lawn, which, incidentally, they've trimmed so perfectly it looks like a photo in a magazine. If they're bookkeepers and male, they'll drive their wives crazy warning them to account for every penny they spend. These same fellows actually seem to enjoy wearing suits with waistcoats, jackets, white shirts and ties. If their wives are as compulsive as they are, they stand a better chance of making their marriages work. But if not, frustrations by the truckload will surely make them miserable.

Being a slob or a neatnik is a learned behaviour; one isn't born with those tendencies. And being learned, both parties are comfortable being what they were taught, just as they're comfortable speaking the languages they were reared to speak. This fact should be considered a fortunate condition because it offers hope that both can change enough to bring a reasonable compromise to the marriage.

Let's not take sides between these two behaviours. It is perfectly possible to live happily and to raise a healthy family whether one is a disorderly person or a perfectionist, even if both parties have the same lifestyle. It's when one is a slob and the other a neatnik that the trouble starts. This isn't often realized while these couples are dating. Or, if they are aware of these differences, it doesn't seem to matter. Love is blind. In time, however, when these small but daily differences add up and go on for months and years, the strain shows.

When I counsel these couples I'm surprised by how few other problems they have in addition to this one over neatness. I've explored their relationships carefully and have reached that conclusion after many sessions. That's why it dawned on me slowly that the issue of neatness wasn't the simple or innocent problem one would normally think it is. From my experience the differences over being neat or casual can tear a marriage apart and change lovers into fighters.

She came to me wanting to know how she could cope with a husband who had two habits she felt she couldn't tolerate. The first was smoking. He would leave cigar butts wherever the thing had to be put out. The smell permeated the house and the husband. Only after he showered and brushed his teeth did she trust his coming close. His clothes reeked of stale cigar smoke so strongly she gagged when she got a noseful.

The second objection was his deplorable messiness. He was one of the most classic slobs I've ever dealt with. Not that he was spiteful nor mean, just poorly bred. When he finished reading the paper he dropped it on the floor next to his chair. His coffee cup stayed on the side table when he was through with it; he didn't take it to the kitchen on his way to the bedroom. He dressed in the bedroom and bathroom and left his discarded clothes wherever he happened to be at the time.

When he left the dining table he left his dishes behind. If asked he would gladly help wash up, or even do them alone, but he never broke his habit of not minding if they weren't washed.

His car was a mess, more like a garbage bin on wheels. Beer cans and fast-food wrappers littered the floor. And of course, it was never washed until his wife took it to the car-wash.

But he was, despite all this filth, a gentle and kind man. He gave his wife all the freedom she could want. He praised her for her good works, her meals and her mothering of their children. The more I probed her for his merits the more she realized his fine qualities. It wasn't long before she came to the inescapable conclusion that she could accept him, more for better than worse. But it wasn't easy. She kept her mind on the prize – a good man despite all his faults – and loved him.

Realistically speaking, this solution isn't for every slob–neatnik couple. Some couples must fight it out issue by issue, and probably compromise on most of them. To do that, six conditions must be avoided. I call five of them the coward-makers. If they can't be mastered, those who drive us crazy are not likely to change their exasperating ways. In addition to five fears which must be mastered, a sixth psychological condition must also be avoided: anger. Let's start with the last first.

Anger

I've already written a book titled *Overcoming Frustration and Anger*. Therefore, I'll only give you a brief version of what you need to know about this subject. It may even be better this way since we tend to remember the basics of a subject, not every nuance of it.

There are, practically speaking, four erroneous beliefs we all make when we get angry:

First, people or things make you angry. Wrong. You make yourself angry because you have bitter thoughts, and a moment later you feel them throughout your body. Don't think mad and don't get mad. Remember also that some days you react to frustration with fury and the next you take the same problem calmly. If that frustration could actually make you upset it would do it every time you were frustrated by it. If you practise questioning the idea that people or things make you angry and you stop thinking that way, the anger stops. It's that simple. Not easy to do, but simple to understand.

The second mistake we make is to believe that if we want something, we have to have it. Wrong. Though it would be delightful if we got everything we wanted, that's not proof that we have to have everything we want. When you get mad you've made your wishes and desires so strong that they can't technically be called wishes any longer. They're called demands. When you change healthy wishes into neurotic demands (and don't get what you insist you should have), that's when you create anger for yourself. Never make another demand and you'll never get angry again.

The only times when getting angry is not neurotic and immature is when it saves someone's life or when you fake it to make people do something automatically for quick results. In the first instance, becoming furious to fight off an attack is perfectly healthy because you will fight better and maybe scare them off. In the second instance, yelling angrily at a child to get him out of the street could save the youngster's life.

The temper tantrum of an adult is no different from the tantrum of a three-year-old child. Kids have fits because they can't tell the difference between wanting something and needing something. They're young and we would expect that from them.

When we adults get angry, however, we regress to the level of a baby each and every time we get mad because we too are telling ourselves we *have* to have everything we want. We're adults, not kids. We don't *have* to have everything we want no matter how right we are. Being right in an argument doesn't justify getting angry, since the other parties are angry at you because they think they're just as right as you do.

Be careful that you don't believe you can't tolerate not getting your way. You *can* stand not getting what you want. If you couldn't you'd die; if you don't die, you've stood it. It's that simple. Yet people tell themselves many times they can't stand to be teased or bullied, and a week later, when they tell me about the incident, they're apparently still alive. So they could stand it after all.

The third mistake angry people make is to believe that when people do something bad, it means they're bad too. Wrong. You can't judge the worth of a person by one or even several acts taken out of a whole lifetime of behaviour, no matter how bad those acts may be. People do negative things because they're deficient, ignorant or disturbed, not because they're evil. We must separate the rating of the person from the rating of the behaviour.

That doesn't mean that just because we forgive people for wrongdoing that we ignore their misdeeds, such as brutality by the bullies or the selfishness of the brats. Those people need to be penalized to help them over their disturbances.

The last mistake angry people make is believing that harsh and cruel treatment turns bad people into good ones. Wrong. It makes them hate their accusers more, they are far less willing to change, or it turns them into low-self-esteem neurotics.

Children in particular have their self-images practically destroyed after being told they're stupid, ugly, or worse. Those words are so powerful to youngsters that they can't think their way around them the way most mature adults can. But when children are hit and theatened, the feeling of being rejected by their mother and father is so devastating that the only explanation that makes sense to them is that they must be very wicked, or why else would their parents treat them so badly? Enough said.

Guilt

If you want to confront crazymakers and get them to respect you, it's essential that you shouldn't feel guilty when you deliberately resist them. If reasoning with them doesn't work, you're left with tough love and firmness. That can bother sensitive souls who've been taught two wrongs don't make a right. True. But when you get tough with troublemakers that's not a wrong, it's an act of love, tough love. That realization is what can give you the freedom to stand up to control freaks, for example. To feel guilty for making someone uncomfortable is to sabotage the very results you are trying to achieve.

Learn instead to distinguish *feeling* guilty from *being* guilty. When you tease children they'll get upset. You've frustrated them, certainly, and for that you *are* guilty. But why must you *feel* guilty, which is the same as hating yourself? Remember the point I made previously? Even if you've done something wrong you have a moral obligation to forgive yourself.

Then, ask yourself if what you've done is actually bad. Standing up to crazymakers is healthy for them and everyone else. Guilt is created in two steps, not one. You first have to do a bad thing, and then you must decide you are also a bad person. Since there are no good or bad people in the world, only good or bad behaviours, you can't logically feel guilty. Making brats unhappy isn't a bad act, but if you thoughtlessly made a mistake and made an innocent person unhappy, you still needn't hate yourself. Remember, you're human and thus imperfect. So, learn by your errors, assert yourself to make others treat you with dignity, and don't feel guilty about it or you will surely end up rewarding bad behaviour.

Other-pity

When you stand put and refuse to let your immature partner or children run the show selfishly you will surely receive tears, cries of hatred, and accusation of injustice. That's done for your benefit in the hope you'll feel guilty and pity those poor, suffering souls because they can't borrow money for a car they haven't earned, or those partners who abused their partner's trust and now want another chance.

When you observe that degree of disturbance in those close to you who need reigning in, be glad. They'd better learn to appreciate what they have and stop being so self-centred. Making them frustrated in order to snap them back to reality is precisely what you've been aiming for. You *want* them to be uncomfortable.

At that precise moment when victory is virtually in hand, guess what often happens? You feel sorry for the discomfort they're going through. The slouched shoulder as the youngster leaves the room after being told he must do homework tonight and can't join his friends, tears at the strings of your heart and you feel sorry for him. Then, horror of horrors, you give in to the poor dear and tell him he can go out after all. The brats win again.

Fear of rejection

I classify this as the greatest fear most people have. We're so hungry to be loved and approved of, we practically stand on our heads not to offend anyone lest they dislike us or not speak to us for three days. Granted, that may be uncomfortable but hardly unbearable. Yet at the mere suspicion that we're likely to be disapproved of we turn into jelly.

Rejection doesn't hurt; it's harmless. All of us experience it many times during our lives and we manage to get through it quite well in most cases. When we don't cope with it well, it's not because we're hurt by the rejection. Rather, it's because we make a big deal of it and talk ourselves into *making* it hurt.

If you don't learn to ignore rejection to the point where you're immobilized, you're doomed to be the slave of others' demands. No matter what bullies or control freaks insist upon, your fear of being thought poorly of will weaken you into submission every time.

Stop believing you need to be loved to be an acceptable person. Who are these people, anyway, who can pass judgement on you? Just because your boss calls you a fool certainly doesn't make you one. What if he called you a bus? Would you believe him? No? Why not? Because you're not made of metal, you don't roll around on wheels, and people don't climb into you for a ride. So, convince yourself that such an accusation is utter nonsense.

Well then, why can't you question all accusations in the same way? Are you told you're a slob, you're stupid, ugly, lazy? Don't take great offence. The accusation is right or wrong. If right, thank your accuser for pointing out your fault and assure that person you'll try your best to change. If it's not true, consider the matter only as a difference of opinion. You surely wouldn't feel rejected if the two of you disagreed over how good a movie was, would you? You thought the film was great. Your partner thought it was a waste of time. So what? A difference of opinion is just that and nothing more. Relax.

Fear of physical and financial harm

These two fears are different from the others because they demand genuine concern. It makes little sense to be afraid of rejection but it makes a great deal of sense to fear physical or financial harm. A woman who's married to an abusive husband (a bully) who may hurt her unless she hops to his commands is in real danger. And a woman who is married to a control freak and is threatened to be penniless unless she does his bidding is also facing considerable danger.

When people face either of these threats they're perfectly rational *not* to resist. I advise they go along with the crazymakers until they can escape, or until the threat passes. However, the best solution for slobs and neatniks lies in compromise: don't make too much of your partner's habits. Look for their good points; count your blessings; don't insist you have to have your way; don't make mountains out of molehills (even if there are piles of dishes in the kitchen, or heaps of clothes in the bedroom corner).

It's quite possible to live with all kinds of weird personalities. All you have to do is to tell yourself several sensible things, such as: a) you don't need to have your own way; b) even if you don't get what you want, that's hardly the end of the world; c) by giving in to your slob or neatnik partner you could be introduced to behaviours which you might find enjoyable – you never know!

Lastly, always remember, nothing disturbs you unless you let it. Living with a crazymaker is very frustrating, as all of us know. But they disturb us only as much as we talk ourselves into. That's true for living with control freaks and bullies, but the job is simply more difficult, that's all. With patience and lots of practice, you can manage these people much better than you presently believe.

Pests and their annoying habits

Among the more common problems people give each other – problems which appear to be nothing more than irritations on the surface – some end up being serious causes of friction. So serious can these annoyances be that violence, arguments, and even divorce might be the consequence. Let me give you several examples of individuals and couples who let themselves become so disturbed over the habits of others that they sought counselling to cope with them.

Every so often men complain strongly about their partners telling them what clothes to wear and when to wear them. Some women tend to be far more conscious of style in dress than men give thought to. Beauty and style are what they live for. They don't hesitate to tell their mates which ties, belts, shirts, and jackets they should wear. The presumption is that their men are socially inadequate and can't possibly make it out there in the real world unless the ladies guide their every step.

Small wonder these men wanted help dealing with this annoyance.

Then there's the fellow who aggravates his partner to the point that she's ready to scream. The fellow exaggerates facts whenever it makes him look better. He makes his wife blush when he tells others of his heroic army exploits, the many famous people he shook hands with, and the money he made and lost on the stockmarket.

A woman once told me of a habit her mother had while driving. She would never pull or push the indicator lever all the way so that it worked without her hand on it. Instead, she would move it just enough to make the indicator point right or left, but she'd keep her hand on it all the while. When my client told her mother she didn't have to do that, and making a turn with both hands on the wheel was easier and safer, the older woman just smiled and reminded her daughter that by lightly touching the lever she wasn't wearing it out as fast.

Another woman feels she can no longer enjoy the company of her boyfriend because he's so pessimistic. He has no confidence in the future or in the goodness of man. When something goes wrong, he imagines the worst, seldom the best. It got so bad she was ready to end their relationship. To avoid this she agreed to counselling to see if it could be saved.

A young man asked for my help in dealing with his father, who corrected his son while driving. His backseat-driving habit almost caused the boy to have an accident. That's all it took to get him to see me. Actually, his father had the annoying habit of correcting his son's dress style, haircut and table manners as well. He was a loving man – the boy never questioned that – but he was a nitpicker, and he drove the boy to the point of confrontation.

Abusive drinkers practically always drive people crazy. They reek of alcohol, they spend money the family needs for rent and food, and they give the family a bad name, what with all their loud and dangerous behaviour, which often wakes up the neighbours.

Other types who infuriate the average person are malcontents. They're grumpy, whingeing and complaining, and must be related to the champion misanthrope of all times – Scrooge.

Or there are those people who almost always answer a question with a question; or cease being affectionate and give no explanation for the change; or try to force their religious or political views on to friends or family; or who need to lose weight, complain about it, but never diet and exercise.

The list could go on and on, but you get the idea. In each of these examples, counselling proved unable to alter the annoying behaviours my clients suffered from. I instructed all parties to assert themselves in the hopes that by going on strike they could discourage their frustrators enough to get them to change. This didn't work. The pests were either so comfortable with their bad habits that they weren't inclined to give them up, or the victims didn't have the stomach to get into nasty power struggles which were sure to follow.

They could have separated themselves from their frustrators through divorce or by simply moving away, but that usually involved additional pain they didn't want to encounter.

On my advice they didn't choose to tolerate these annoyances with resentment since that would have led to any number of symptoms including anger, depression and low self-esteem. Instead, I taught them to tolerate the behaviour *without* resentment. I explained to them that neurotics must behave like neurotics; pessimists have to be nay-sayers; backseat drivers will go on giving instructions on how fast to drive, when to switch lanes, etc.; those who won't diet will rationalize that they're not that heavy, dieting is too hard or being thin is unhealthy; spendthrifts will deny they're careless with money, or that gambling will win back all they lost; incompetent workers will be incompetent.

In short, to live with difficult people – let's call them neurotics – people who aren't stupid but who behave stupidly – you need to observe the following two pieces of advice.

First, don't expect people to do what they can't for the present do. If your partner is struggling with alcohol abuse, don't expect him or her to come home smelling of perfume or with a pocket full of money. Get real: abusive drinkers abuse alcohol. That's what abusive drinkers do. If they could stop they wouldn't abuse alcohol.

In the same vein, jealous people have to protest your enjoying the company of others. To insist they shouldn't be jealous is tantamount to saying jealous people shouldn't be jealous. Remember again, if they could control that feeling they wouldn't be jealous neurotics.

Tolerate what you can't change; it's easier than pushing water uphill. Remind yourself that nothing upsets you unless you let it. Then, remind yourself that you *can* accept discomfort. You're an adult, a grown-up. You've put up with millions of frustrations already, and you'll face millions more in the years ahead. Then, stop being angry with the pests in your life. They aren't bad. They're human and have a right to be neurotic, stupid and annoying.

Also don't forget, you're no different than the pests you're pulling your hair out for. You're as human as they, and you bother people in your unique way, just as others do in their particular way.

The second insight you'll want to understand is this: don't take the annoying habits of others personally. Whatever you're dealing with is no different than what the pest does to others.

The partner who goes to bed at 2 am and gets up at 1 pm isn't doing that just to you. Night-owls are night-owls, that's all. They do that to whoever they live with. Just imagine what would happen if you were snatched out of that relationship and were replaced with someone else. In one month the pest would be treating that person in the same way you were treated. The drinking, the jealousy, the backseat driving and the pessimism would all come back in their full glory.

Realizing this, how can you possibly take pests personally? Instead, ignore their behaviour gracefully and get on with your life with serenity. Life is too short to waste it fighting those you live and work with. Instead, detach yourself therapeutically, decide they're somewhat eccentric, mind your own business, and let them spoil their own lives if they won't listen to your advice.

7

Finishing touches

As I reflect on what I've written in the previous chapters, I'm not unmindful of the impression these pages may have made on the sensibilities of many of my readers. I have focused on the ugly traits of people, not their merits. I've urged you to put aside your gentle and patient ways as you deal with these difficult people in the full knowledge that many of you will probably feel uncomfortable being tough on your family, partners or friends.

All of our lives we've been taught to turn the other cheek, to love those who do us wrong, that two wrongs do not make a right and that we are our brothers keepers. How then do I expect you to take seriously my recommendations which instruct you to turn the other cheek only twice if the party in question doesn't know he or she did wrong? And if the party already knew that what he or she did was unacceptable, I have, hopefully, urged you not to turn your cheek even once. And worse yet, I've actually urged you to treat those who abuse you with similar degrees of discomfort, not show them tolerance or affection.

What all this comes down to is this: I firmly believe that the common views of how to deal with people come from religious views formulated ages before the modern era of psychology. Those teachings were harsh, frightening and mentally unhealthy to the point of creating great emotional suffering. Hell, fire and brimstone were realities to people in the Middle Ages, not to be taken lightly.

To me it's only natural that the passage of time would reveal new insights to each new generation, and that knowledge is never complete. Those of you who are confused by my views will be relieved to learn that what I've offered isn't a complete departure from present spiritual views. Instead, they're essential refinements to the views most of us were reared with. These modifications are only few in number, but none the less important.

If we follow the changes I have suggested, the world will improve. The benefits will be twofold: we ourselves will gain greater control over those disturbances which have plagued people for thousands of years. But more, as we grow morally and psychologic-ally we will deal with the difficult people in our lives first with appreciation, then with patience and understanding, and, finally, with firmness when necessary.

These are the tools we must use if we're to achieve cooperation, respect and love. They represent degrees of sacrifice. From some we expect a minimal sacrifice when we ask someone to give us directions. If we need to leave our children for a whole afternoon because we must visit a family member in hospital, we hope our neighbour will make the moderate sacrifice and care for our children for a few hours. That's more than cooperation – it shows compassion and a willingness to be frustrated to a degree we only show people who we feel good about, who we respect.

Love requires the greatest sacrifice of all. All of the wage earner's income is shared, time is reduced to one's sports or leisure activities in order to serve our partners and children, and if we must lose our lives to save a child or partner, that is a choice love expects us to make.

None of this should be new to you. What we may not agree on is how we achieve those benefits. Customary belief has it that if we want cooperation, respect and love we should please people so much that they'll feel obligated to the point where they can't refuse us. Not only that, but, if we've been exceptionally kind, we'll supposedly make others feel so deeply for us that they'll deny us nothing!

I wish it were so. Not that this view is all wrong. It isn't. It works that way only with mature and/or undisturbed people. When we deal with the opposite – immature and/or disturbed persons – those lofty ideals fail. That's what modern psychology has clearly concluded. When dealing with the immature or disturbed group we make things worse when we turn the other cheek.

Some of the crazymakers I described in the previous pages are born with genes which tend toward violence or emotional upsets. Others are trained that way. They learned to control, fight and manipulate families and friends who thought they were being helpful by being so tolerant (loving), but who actually trained others to be emotionally disturbed. And one of the biggest mistakes they made was to reward the very behaviour they protested.

Can you imagine such a turn of events? We, the dominant culture, have indirectly been creating the behaviours we disapprove of the most. The result is that there seems no let-up in the number of difficult people we all encounter. A change in our understanding of difficult people is clearly called for, and then a change in how we deal with them must follow. The change is basically: do not reinforce negative behaviour.

To accomplish this we must accept the three principles of human interaction, which explain how we get problems with people, and the three rules of assertion, which explain what we must do to correct those problems. In addition, however, you need to know if you have strong objections to those ideas. If so, they must be realized and removed or change remains impossible.

The three principles of human interaction

1 You get the behaviour you tolerate.
2 Others will not change unless you change first.
3 Control your excessive toleration.

The three rules of assertion

1 If people do something good to you, do something good to them $(+ = +)$.
2 If people do something bad to you, and don't realize they're behaving badly, reason with them, but only on two separate occasions $(- = + \times 2)$.
3 If people are inconsiderate a third time, do something equally annoying to them, but it must be without anger, guilt, other-pity, fear of rejection, fear of physical harm or fear of financial harm $(- = -)$.

If you have objections to my programme for change, they'll probably be in the form of the following complaints.

First objection: two wrongs don't make a right. This is an understandable objection, to be sure. And it's absolutely correct whenever we deal with two wrongs. However, when we return one discomfort with another, and do it with the intention of helping others correct their inconsiderate habits, then our responses can't be considered wrong or bad. If our efforts stop bad habits and lead to their correction as well, then whatever pain we have used must be thought of as a good thing.

All of you who protest this argument but who have children will have to assure me you've never made your children uncomfortable after they've behaved badly. If you've spanked, scolded or denied them in order to wake them up to the realization that they've behaved unacceptably, then you're guilty of returning one wrong with another. At least that's how the children viewed your response. From your point of view, you behaved lovingly and responsibly even though firmly. Though it may have hurt you more than your child, you did it nevertheless. So convinced were you, if they misbehaved and talking to them twice about it didn't help, that nothing was left for you to do but to return one wrong with an act which you knew to be right, but which was viewed by the child as a monstrous wrong.

The third rule of assertion tells us that to discourage bad behaviour we must offer something equally discomforting in return. To do otherwise is tantamount to encouraging misbehaviour. This is clearly one of the major reasons for so much emotional disturbance, immaturity and immoral behaviour in our society today. We have clearly been rewarding behaviour through our well-meant toleration.

In summary, when someone does something mean to you and does it with anger and with selfish motives behind his actions, that's wrong. When you do a painful thing to *help* someone get over his immoral or disturbed ways, then that becomes a good. It isn't the act itself which is moral or immoral, it's the intention behind the act – to hurt or to help – which determines its moral and ethical status.

Second objection: if we don't turn the other cheek we're being motivated by revenge, nothing less. And that's totally wrong. 'Vengeance is mine, sayeth the Lord.' Precisely. Vengeance is an ugly, neurotic emotion which I in no way uphold. The third rule of assertion states that, reasoning, having failed on two occasions, we must then return one pain for another of equal intensity. However, – and this makes all the difference – it must be applied without anger, hatred or vengeance. Otherwise, that would make rule number three a definition of aggression, not assertion.

When we stand up for our rights with anger we're being aggressive. When we stand up for our rights without anger we're being assertive.

Third objection: it forces us to lower ourselves to the level of those who offend us. True enough. But it can't be helped. How nice it would be if we could all discuss our differences with one another over a cup of tea and biscuits, calmly offering our views after quietly and patiently listening to complaints against us. There are only a few of us capable of such elegant conduct. However, even if we could all remain calm and make our points in lofty, abstract terms, we would still be highly ineffective.

Communication is never effective if we don't speak the language of the listener. To speak with children or foreigners our discourse almost automatically goes to their level. What do we do, however, when we've made our case as clearly as we can without results? If we continue to reason with our frustrators we do nothing less than reinforce the very behaviour we're exclaiming against.

In short, words are then irrelevant to the crazymakers. They don't take them seriously, or they don't comprehend the nature of their wrongful actions. To communicate at all we must take a different path, one which will surely be understood: actions, not words. Ultimately, all living things respond to pain or discomfort. So we lower ourselves to the action level, which they can't reason against or argue their way out of. The employee who's been warned twice to arrive at work on time may finally get the message when he's politely sent home for the day if he's tardy the third time.

Objection four: it's too much like playing games. Granted, it does appear to be so at first glance. The tit-for-tat design of rule three can easily be interpreted as a silly game, beneath the standards of mature adults. For instance, if you keep me waiting repeatedly, I will, after speaking to you about this twice, keep you waiting the next opportunity I have. Sounds immature, doesn't it? Not so. If I'm troubled by your inconsiderate treatment of me and I do nothing about it, I'll learn to dislike you. Furthermore, I'll indirectly be teaching you to be inconsiderate to others. This isn't a game, I assure you. Games are fun. This is serious stuff and has consequences for good or bad, depending on our reactions.

How will you know if the issue in question is serious? If you resent the action, take it seriously and respond in kind. To do less places you below the just-reasonable-content level, and that will lead to neurotic symptoms such as depression, anger or anxiety.

Love and forgiveness

What is the place of love and forgiveness in this scheme of things? Doubtlessly the thought has occurred to you that my approach is cold and unforgiving. You will have observed that I tolerate nonsense only twice if the individual doesn't realize the behaviour is wrong, unethical or immoral. And I don't tolerate it even the first time if it's clear that the person already knows the behaviour to be wrong or highly inconsiderate.

Such an approach seems to shock people as uncaring, unfeeling and just plain mean. But I maintain that those who repeatedly warn others about their thoughtless acts, and who seldom do anything but talk about their complaints, are the real and truly unfeeling and uncaring people. The father who repeatedly tells his son not to swear at his mother is conditioning the boy to disrespect her if the father eventually doesn't take the boy by the ear or take away his privileges.

Such refusal to act, to risk a scene, to risk rejection from his son, to risk giving the young man a neurotic problem is the result of ignorance about human development and a misunderstanding as to what true love is all about. That youngster needs to be taught to control his speech, to appreciate what his parents have sacrificed for him and that he doesn't need to have everything he wants. If his father doesn't make a change, his son won't change, at least not until he is about 30 years old.

When the father penalizes his son's rude behaviour he's showing the boy true love because to become a moral and decent person such behaviour towards one's parents should never be tolerated. Were this father to follow my programme of assertion he would be showing his son mature and caring love, not based on indulgence but on correction, and he would be teaching the boy how to create love from others for himself.

Most people believe they show how much they love someone by how much they do for them: 'If you truly love me you'd do what I ask,' is the way they're taught to understand love. I make the point that mature and lasting love is also demonstrated by what we don't do for others. The young adult who lives with his parents while looking for a job may ultimately have to be given a deadline and told his bags will be on the doorstep if he isn't employed and housed elsewhere within a month.

Giving the significant others in our lives everything they ask for is like giving a baby all the sweets he or she demands. It can lead to emotional and physical disorders. So much for indulgence as a measure of love.

Unconditional love

Indulged people, especially the brats, have all been raised with too much unconditional love. This is another of the huge mistakes being made in our culture today: that loving people unconditionally is an act of the highest love. That, ladies and gentlemen, is a classic delusion, except in the case of young children, feeble adults and pets. All others are being abused, if loved unconditionally. Why? Because no distinction is made between acceptable and unacceptable behaviour. Therefore we end up either punishing and rewarding negative actions, or punishing and rewarding positive actions. Surely that's a formula for bedlam.

Look what happens when a man routinely gets drunk at family gatherings and then quarrels with his daughter-in-law. In time, she finds this intolerable and refuses to participate in future family affairs, much to the annoyance of her husband. He in turn feels he has to attend – he loves his father right or wrong – and feels his wife is mean to expect him to confront the elder gentleman.

This is a typical and classic case of unconditional love. No matter what grandfather does, he gets away with it. No one, in my opinion, loves him enough to put up with his future rejection, his counterattacks and his attempts to cause his accusers to feel his wrath and blame by confronting him. They tolerate both his immature and immoral behaviour no less than his mature and moral behaviour.

The problem is that they don't know how to be intolerant and assertive while at the same time being loving and forgiving. Actually, they don't know how to love and don't know how to forgive. Neither of these states are simple or easy to understand and/or to practise.

My definition of love goes as follows: 'Love is that powerful feeling you have for someone or something that has, is, or will satisfy your deepest desires and needs.' There it is again, the idea that we love people, animals or things as long as they please us in important ways. But that isn't entirely correct either. When we say we love someone what we more accurately mean is that we love a number of very specific qualities, traits or habits that person has. You may love your adolescent son's sense of humour or his good looks; but you may hate his arrogance and disrespect for authority, the way he dresses or has his hair cut. If the boy has many more lovable qualities than undesirable ones, it makes sense to say you love your son out of practical considerations. Actually, you don't love the whole person, you love the positive things about the boy, not technically the boy.

In the same vein, if your son were a gangster, beat his wife and molested his children, and possessed a great number of other ugly characteristics you would feel you hated your son. Again, however, you would be ignoring the boy's fine qualities. Technically you would hate the negative habits, not the son.

You don't know it – most people don't – but you can't logically love or hate anyone. You can only love or hate elements of a person: the way he washed his own dishes Wednesday morning at 7:36 am – ten minutes later you may have disapproved of him for leaving the light on in his bedroom before going to school.

Taken to its logical conclusion, this means we don't love or hate anyone. It also means there are no good or bad people in the world, only good or bad behaviours or characteristics. Is this possible? Am I being serious? Absolutely, and let me show you again why.

1　You surely wouldn't rate someone on the basis of a single act, would you? Is a great singer great in all other respects also? Is a murderer bad in all other respects?

2　If we can't judge people on the basis of one major trait, we can't do it by several either. There are millions of judgements we can make about any person. Every deed and thought over a lifetime would have to be considered if we were to make a valid rating of any person.

3　We can't agree on what is a good or bad trait.

4　Even if we could, they would change as we did the evaluation since it would take years to gather all the data.

To rate a person good or bad we would have to add up all the positive points about a person and then subtract all the negative ones. If we came out with more good ratings you could say that was a good person.

Since such incredibly minute and detailed studies are never likely to be made, we're simply not permitted to rate anyone in such global terms. Only very detailed ratings are valid. This being so, it further begs another conclusion. We must forgive everyone for everything since there are no bad people, only bad habits. One of the finest lines

I ever wrote is from my book *Overcoming Frustration and Anger*: 'Forgive everything, forget nothing.' This is the same sentiment expressed in the Bible when it advises us to 'forgive seventy-times-seven'. That I agree with totally. No one is bad, only fallible. We're reminded frequently that we're all sinners. Of course we are, otherwise we would have to be perfect.

The moral teachings most of us were exposed to as children taught us one major idea: we must love one another unconditionally. This is pointed out in such common expressions as turn the other cheek, or that we must forgive seventy-times-seven, clearly implying that we must forgive everything. And by forgiving everything we're showing unconditional love.

Society took these teachings to heart and achieved a milestone in its treatment of its citizens. The belief that we were all deserving of forgiveness, regardless of our faults, ran completely counter to the belief that some of us are bad and deserve great suffering for our misdeeds.

As noble as that forward step was, some harm has resulted from the way these teachings were understood and applied. As psychology in particular has studied human behaviour, it now is perfectly clear that a correction in these moral teachings is called for.

Our present misunderstanding of these principles, though we adhere to them with the best of intentions, has at times led to disastrous consequences. Loving and caring parents have unwittingly taught some children to hate themselves over their errors or to disrespect the parents who indulged the children with assurances of unconditional love. But let me address the former error first: using guilt to correct behaviour. Thereafter, I shall explain the dangers of turning the other cheek, the psychology of forgiveness and what true unconditional love means.

Guilt is created in two steps: first, you did something bad, and second, you conclude you too are bad. In short, you have been taught that there are good and bad people in the world, not just good and bad habits. You need to make a distinction between being guilty and feeling guilty.

You *are* guilty when you steal money from your company. You did the robbing, others didn't. For this you will hopefully suffer legal consequences and pay your debt to society with a fine or a jail sentence. To do less would be tantamount to rewarding you for your crime.

So far so good. I'm sure you find nothing wrong with my analysis up to this point. However, I'll now make another point, but this one will be more difficult for most of you to accept. It says that, even though you're guilty of a wrongdoing, doesn't mean you have to *feel* guilty also.

Feeling guilty is the same as hating yourself. Your esteem drops, your sense of inferiority mounts, you need to hurt yourself physically, socially, vocationally or psychologically to atone for your evil ways. Unfortunately, we do not usually achieve good behaviour through self-hate.

We have a moral obligation to forgive ourselves for any undesirable act, not because we're bad, but because we're imperfect. Human beings, being human, fall short of perfection in millions of ways, from murder, rape, pillage and plunder just to mention a few of the major imperfections. What about the minor ones, such as greed, jealousy, dishonesty, laziness and pride? Yes, those too.

There are three reasons we can use to forgive ourselves of any wrong while at the same time paying the consequences of our wrong acts. In fact, I believe we all have a moral right – I prefer to think we have a moral obligation – to forgive ourselves of any wicked acts since they're the result of deficiency, ignorance and disturbance.

Much pain is created because we all have areas of considerable deficiency. A boy can't understand maths. A girl can't hum a tune. You can't dance to a beat, and your friend can't draw a straight line. Some of us are born extroverts and make friends wherever we go; some are born introverts and avoid parties like the plague.

In one form or another we're all deficient. This leads to making mistakes when we have trouble adding numbers. It leads to accidents when we have nervous systems which confuse us when we want to turn left but end up turning right.

To hate yourself for not being able to do something which is impossible for you is the height of conceit. You aren't God, who could be perfect under any conditions. You're human and filled with many shortcomings. When you do something negative, it isn't the fault of your being evil, it's the fault of your being deficient.

The second reason you have a moral obligation to forgive yourself is ignorance. All of us are ignorant in many ways. If your baby dies because you didn't know how to get it breathing again, forgive yourself: you were ignorant. If you're fired from your job because you kept improper records, forgive yourself: you didn't know precisely which records the company wanted. If you had an accident while driving your friend's new car, forgive yourself: just as you needed to signal your turn you indicated the wrong direction because you didn't know how to work the signal in a car you had never driven.

Ignorance is a perfectly legitimate reason for not hating yourself. What you don't know you can't be expected to show.

The last reason why you have a moral obligation to forgive yourself is: disturbance. When you abuse a child, have a car accident after a screaming encounter with the family, get furious and smash furniture, or fail to appear for work because you drank too much the night before, you are behaving badly because you were disturbed. How else is a disturbed person supposed to behave?

You have an ethical and moral right to accept yourself as a fallible human being who frequently does dumb things because of deficiency, ignorance or disturbance. When you do that you free up your brain to understand what you've done and why, and what you might do to avoid those actions again. To do otherwise invites guilt, depression, low self-esteem and a deep need to hurt yourself for weeks, months or years to come. It's your choice.

Forgiveness

There's a great deal of confusion over this word. Yet it has one meaning only and that's a simple one. In the final analysis, forgiveness comes down to this: when you object to a person's behaviour but you're not angry with the person, that's forgiveness.

The elimination of the anger is the key issue. To say you forgive someone but you still hold a grudge, or you want revenge doesn't make sense. Only when anger is totally avoided is it possible to claim forgiveness.

This is crucial to achieve if we're to have healthy and compatible relationships. Those who fail to achieve forgiveness do so for several reasons. They believe people who do bad things are themselves bad and thus need to be punished. And what better way than to hold a grudge for years?

Or, forgiveness can be withheld because people are so thin-skinned that they take needlessly strong offence over an innocent act which others manage to overlook in a matter of minutes (or hours at the most), but which they can't get over in years.

To achieve forgiveness, the skill of talking yourself out of anger is essential. Being firm and kind (another way of defining assertion) is the best answer. How different this is from the way most people express forgiveness. They think that to forgive someone, they must give in to that person's wishes.

Take the case of an adolescent girl who wears her mother's sweaters to school every so often, despite the protestations from the mother. Finally getting her fill of such inconsiderate behaviour the mother takes away the use of the family car from the girl.

The girl sees the trouble she's in and tells mother she is sorry, clearly asking for forgiveness. At this point her mother has to make a critical choice: to get over her anger and let the girl have the car back, or to get over the anger and not let her have the car back.

The latter is, of course, the sensible way to deal with this issue and others like it. The girl is likely to exclaim, however, 'But, mum, I thought you forgave me?' And the mother has every right to respond, 'Sweetheart, I do forgive you. I'm not angry with you. I fully understand how tempted you were to wear my sweater. You looked beautiful in it. However, you knew I didn't allow it, I spoke to you a number of times about it and you refused to obey. Therefore, I'm not going to lift my grounding you from the use of the car. I need to make sure you've learned your lesson.' That, folks, is good psychology, and moral behaviour as well.

The other cheek

Most people confuse tolerance with forgiveness. In fact, that's how they define forgiveness. 'I forgive you for keeping me waiting, so let's forget this now and have a good time.' Such a conversation suggests you haven't remained angry for being made to wait, and it also shows us that you want to forget it as well.

We do this because we want to show our love and to be loved. And that's not all bad. But a little tolerance goes a long way. Repeatedly tolerating unkind behaviour in an attempt to show how forgiving you can be leads to some of the worst habits I've come across in my long career as a psychologist.

Another way to express this practice is known as 'turning the other cheek'. It sounds like a gentle and decent thing to do, and that it would unmistakably lead to warm and loving relationships. Unfortunately such isn't the case after people have had their negative acts tolerated twice. And that very practice of turning the other cheek, giving warning after warning, lecture after lecture, is the very source of a great deal of disturbed behaviour.

If you were looking for a powerful and simple method to ruin a person's character, you couldn't do much better than to forgive and forget. Why is this so? Because you would be rewarding bad behaviour over and over. Whatever you reinforce grows stronger. If you praise someone for interrupting you, don't be surprised to see that happen more often. If you give your son a car after he comes home having failed four exams, you teach him to be lazy.

It's one thing to turn the other cheek once or twice. But watch out for thrice. At that point you're asking for trouble. If you want to be loving in a real and meaningful sense, love others conditionally. Make them earn your love. Don't help them become irresponsible, rude or immature. Reward them when they act in moral and mature ways.

A good share of the trouble with the crazymakers in the world is as a result of our teaching them to be so through our forgiving and forgetting. We forgive, not by tolerating evil, but by not being angry over evil. However, then we get back to work on the evil and use penalties to discourage it rather than use rewards which encourage it.

On second thought, I may have been hasty to describe my system as depending on conditional love. If we define love as what we do to satisfy people's needs rather than only deep desires, then I see no reason why we can't say we should love people with unconditional positive regard. However, to do that we must see all people as basically decent and worthy, and who deserve our love and caring.

I believe we're our brothers keepers. We're all human, trying to get through life as best we can. Some of us have it soft, others have it hard. Some of us turned out civil, others not. No matter, we're all kin, more like each other than any other living thing.

To sum up, when we deal with people's deep desire we're helping them more if we forgive and don't forget. We want to love them on the condition that they've earned our love. But when we're dealing with people's needs, we want to forgive and forget, in other words, to be unconditionally loving. It's then that we sacrifice one of our kidneys to a child who has been rude and inconsiderate. The young man needs a kidney, he'll die without it, so we lay aside all negative feelings which we would normally use to correct his behaviour. Then, when he's recovered from his near-fatal condition and he is rude again, we make our love for him conditional and ground him from using the car for a month.

See the difference? Let's always distinguish these two forms of love and apply them wisely. Perhaps, as a result, we'll reduce the number of crazymakers in our lives, or at least make them much less difficult to be with.

References and further reading

Cooper, K. (1972) *The New Aerobics*, New York: Bantam Books.
Ellis, A. and Hayer, R. (1975) *A New Guide to Rational Living*, North Hollywood, CA: Wilshire Books.
Hauck, P. (1974) *Overcoming Frustration and Anger*, Louisville, KY: Westminster Press.
Hauck, P. (1991) *Overcoming the Rating Game*, London: Sheldon Press.
London, T. (1991) *Managing Anger*, Evanston, IL: Garfield Press.